SCOUTING DOLLS

through the years

IDENTIFICATION AND VALUE GUIDE

Girl Scout HANDBOOK

SYDNEY ANN SUTTON

WITH

PATSY MOYER

cb

COLLECTOR BOOKS

A Division of Schroeder Publishing Co., Inc.

Front cover: 19" composition Effanbee Patsy Ann, circa 1929+, wears a factory-made Girl Scout uniform tagged "DOLLY TOGS//MELROSE, MASS." Patsy Ann shoes are replaced; $900.00 with 1930s Girl Scout handbook ($35.00) and brown lunch box ($100.00).

Note:
Fluffy, Skippy, Patsy Ann, and Suzette are trademarks of Effanbee Doll Company. Barbie, Becky, and Skipper are trademarks of Mattel. Terri Lee is the trademark of the Terri Lee Company.

Cover design by Beth Summers
Book design by Mary Ann Hudson

COLLECTOR BOOKS
P.O. Box 3009
Paducah, Kentucky 42002-3009

www.collectorbooks.com

Copyright © 2003 Sydney Ann Sutton with Patsy Moyer

The current values in this book should be used only as a guide. They are not intended to set prices, which vary from one section of the country to another. Auction prices as well as dealer prices vary greatly and are affected by condition as well as demand. Neither the authors nor the publisher assumes responsibility for any losses that might be incurred as a result of consulting this guide.

Searching For A Publisher?

We are always looking for people knowledgeable within their fields. If you feel that there is a real need for a book on your collectible subject and have a large comprehensive collection, contact Collector Books.

Contents

Effanbee Suzettes, pg. 60

Acknowledgments

Lifelong Girl Scout enthusiast Sydney Ann Sutton with her husband Lawrence and daughter Christine.

First, I want to thank my husband, Lawrence, for all his belief in and support of me in writing this book. A special thank you to Jeannie DuChateau Niswonger for constantly encouraging me to write. Thank you to Lynne Armstrong, Becky Byrns, Randi Cox, Mary Eskridge, Susan Girardot, Judith Izen, Diane Milla, Diane Miller, Pidd Miller, Patsy Moyer, Carolyn Nestrick, Nancy Nunn, Donnie Oldhan, and Bob Trowbridge for use of their photographs or allowing me to photograph part of their collections. A thank you to my children, Lawrence, Jr., Victoria, and Christine, for all the extra housework you did so I could write.

A very special daughter Christine Sutton, who is a Gold Award and Lifetime Girl Scout, shown here at age seventeen wearing an original 1934 Girl Scout uniform ($125.00) and holding composition Effanbee 19" Patsy Ann costumed in a commercially-made 1934 Girl Scout uniform.

A special thank you to Chad Vinson for his hard work photographing the dolls.

Foreword

Over the years, I have met several very active doll collectors who have focused their attention on Girl Scout dolls because of their childhood experiences as members of the Girl Scout organization. When Sydney Ann Sutton told me she wanted to write a book documenting all the various dolls, I had no idea that there was such a variety of dolls and that Girl Scout dolls had been made for such a length of time. Not really aware of the beginnings of the Girl Scout, Girl Guide, and Campfire Girl movements and being a history buff, I immediately was taken by the story of how these organizations came about, who were the people involved, and how the groups were structured. I was also amazed at the number of dolls that have been located, researched, identified, and categorized in this fascinating collecting niche. I think your interest, too, will be piqued by this unique doll collection, *Scouting Dolls Through the Years*, and you will be pleased to add this volume to your research library.

Patsy Moyer

Coleco Cabbage Patch Kids, p. 73

Introduction

In the 1950s, as a child from a dysfunctional family, I had two personal sources of strength and comfort. My Terri Lee doll was my best friend and understood what went on in my family. Girl Scouts was my guide to life. I still try to live by the promise and the laws. I learned the basics of my moral character from Scouting and feel every girl should have a chance to be a Scout. I have been a Brownie, a Junior Scout, a Senior Scout, and a Scout Leader and am proud to be a lifetime member of the Girl Scouts of America. This book has been a ten-year labor of love, in tribute to this organization.

This history of Girl Scout dolls is dedicated to all Girl Scout doll collectors to help them know more about their dolls.

In most examples, the dates placed with the official dolls have come directly from Girl Scout National Equipment catalogs. In some instances, the dolls may have been available a couple of years before or after the catalog that I have. Also the dolls may have been in stock for a few years after they were discontinued from active production.

Some dolls have been dated directly from doll company or fashion catalogs such as Effanbee, Nancy Ann Storybook, Ginny, Ginger, and

Terri Lee Fashion Parades. I have also used J.C. Penney, Sears Roebuck and Co., and Montgomery Ward retail catalogs to date others. These references were also used to make sure the dolls were all original. This author has made every effort to insure accuracy.

The pricing comes from doll shows, dealers, and online auctions. The majority of the dolls shown are mint, so the values given will be accordingly high. Played-with dolls and those with missing items will be valued lower. Value ranges are used for dolls that are probably more available and therefore can be found in varying states of collectible condition.

In order to become familiar with the dolls they collect and how to become a member of a club, contact:

United Federation of Doll Clubs, Inc.
10920 North Ambassador Drive, Suite 130
Kansas City, MO 64153
Website: http://www.ufdc.org/

Terri Lee, p. 40.

Girl Scout History

Juliette Gordon Low, a natural leader. She changed the lives of thousands of girls with the revolutionary idea that girls could do anything. Today the Girl Scouts and Girl Guides continue to touch the lives of girls in many countries.

Juliette Gordon was born October 31, 1860, in Savannah, Georgia, to William Washington Gordon and Eleanor Lytle Kinzie Gordon. Her father was born in 1834 to William Washington Gordon (1796 – 1842) and Sarah Anderson Stites (1808 – 1882). Her grandfather Stites was a member of the Georgia legislature, mayor of Savannah, and founder of the Central Railroad and Banking Company. Her grandfather Gordon was the son of Ambrose Gordon (1751 – 1804) of Monmouth County, N.J., and Elizabeth Meade Gordon. Her father attended Yale and was a lawyer, cotton merchant, and state legislator. Her mother, nicknamed "Nelly," was born in 1835, and died in 1917. Nelly's mother, Juliette Augusta Magill, married John Harris Kinzie of Chicago. She wrote a book about the Chicago Massacre that was published in 1844.

In the Gordon family, Juliette was nicknamed "Daisy" and spent a happy youth in a large home, now a historical landmark, the Juliette Gordon Low Girl Scout National Center. Juliette was interested in the arts, writing, drawing, acting, painting, and sculpting. She attended private schools in Virginia and later a French school in New York City. She traveled in Europe as well as the United States, as she had relatives in Chicago and New Jersey. She also spent time in New York City and at various resorts.

Daisy had three sisters, Eleanor (Nell) born two years before her in 1858; Sarah Alice, born in 1863; and Mabel McLane, born after Daisy. Nell married Richard Wayne Parker and lived in New Jersey and Washington, D.C, where Parker was a Congressman. Mabel married Rowland Charles Frederick Leigh and lived in England where she was honored for her relief work during World War I.

During a mother-daughter trip to New York City in 1880, Alice became very ill with scarlet

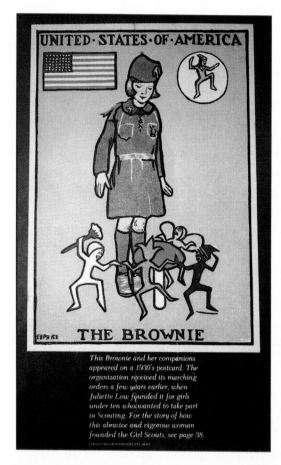

The back cover of the 1928 American Heritage magazine pictures "The Brownie." *Courtesy Lynne Armstrong.*

fever. Nelly sent the other girls home, but seventeen-year-old Alice died in New York in late December. The mother was greatly affected by the death of her third daughter.

Daisy also had two younger brothers, William Washington, Jr., born in 1866, and George Arthur Gordon, born in 1872. Both brothers went to Yale; William became a lawyer and Arthur worked in the family cotton business. Arthur was a confidant of Daisy's, and he and Mabel also frequently wrote back and forth.

Juliette developed hearing problems in her mid-twenties and became deaf in her left ear. She struggled with hearing problems in her right ear for the rest of her life. Daisy was personable, charming, and witty, but also very stubborn. She may have been a bit spoiled, growing up in a comfortably successful family that offered her many opportunities. In a letter to her parents in 1875, at 15 years old, she indicated she did not want to be listed as Juliette in her school annual, but rather as Daisy.

Ten years later, Juliette visited some school friends, the Low sisters, in England, and began seeing their brother William "Willie" Mackay Low. Willie had attended schools in England and was a close friend of Edward, Prince of Wales. Later Juliette was presented twice at court to Queen Victoria.

Willie's father was Andrew Low, a wealthy Scotsman who had inherited wealth from his uncle, and the family had a home on Lafayette Square in Savannah built in 1849, as well as an estate in England. He was a cotton factor and had business dealings with Daisy's father, who was also a cotton factor.

Daisy married Willie on December 12, 1885, and believed she had not only a wonderful, handsome husband, but one who was wealthy as well. She lived part time in England but came back to the United States often to the house on Lafayette Square given to them by Willie's father. During the Spanish American War, Daisy helped her mother start a hospital in Florida for convalescing soldiers. Her father, who had fought for the Confederacy during the Civil War, was stationed in Florida as an Army General during this later conflict. After the war, Daisy returned to England.

Her marriage turned out not to be a very happy one. Her husband indulged in gambling, liquor, and extramarital affairs, and she considered a divorce as early as 1902, but Willie conveniently died in 1905. After his death, Daisy continued to travel and met Sir Robert Baden-Powell, the founder of the Boy Scouts in England. She corresponded with him in 1911 and met his sister Miss Agnes Baden-Powell, who had organized the Girl Guides, an organization for girls modeled after her brother's prototype. Daisy started a Girl Guide troop in Scotland where she spent that summer.

The next spring, on March 12, 1912, Juliette Gordon Low started the first Girl Guides troop in the United States with 18 members, among them her niece, Margaret Daisy Gordon. A Tenderfoot Pin, the trefoil, was chosen to be the logo for this American troop, and in 1913, "Girl Scouts" became the new name.

After World War I, Juliette Low turned over the day-to-day running of the Scouts to others and went to work combining all the Guides and Scouts together as sisters. Her dream was a friendly world brought together by Girl Scouts and Girl Guides. The World Association of Girl Guides and Girl Scouts (WAGGGS), established in 1928 by the International Council of Girl Guides and Girl Scouts, was one of her greatest accomplishments.

As the group began, W. Hoxie wrote the first Girl Scout handbook, *How Girls Can Help Their Country*, and the first national headquarters was located in Washington, D.C. The August 1912 *Ladies' Home Journal* featured a cover by Harrison Fisher showing Girl Guides in white middy blouses and navy bloomers paddling a canoe. Each year brought exciting developments for the young organization.

In 1914, the trefoil symbol was patented and became the official membership logo for American girls. The Girl Scouts could earn 22 badges in different fields and in 1915, the Girl Scouts claimed 5,000 members in 200 troops. Juliette Low reportedly sold her pearls to help support the Girl Scout movement, and the organization held its first annual convention in Washington, D.C. where the group adopted a constitution and bylaws. At that convention, Juliette Gordon Low was elected national president for the years 1915 – 1920. Annual membership dues at this time were 25 cents.

During Juliette Low's tenure as president, the national headquarters was moved to its current home in New York City. The Golden Eaglet award was introduced, and the first Brownie group was organized in Marblehead, Massachusetts. In 1917, First Lady Mrs. Woodrow Wilson became the first honorary president of the Girl Scouts, a tradition which continues today. The Girl Scouts monthly publication of "The Rally" began, the first troop for physically disabled girls was organized in New York, and the first National Training School for Girl Scout leaders was started in Boston.

In 1918, the letters "GS" were added to the design of the Girl Scout pin. In 1919, work toward an International Council of Girl Guides and Girl Scouts began. The organization produced a public service motion picture about Girl Scouts, "The Golden Eaglet," a black-and-white silent film which premiered in New York City's Fine Arts Theater on January 16. Girl Scout Week was first celebrated and was instituted for the future to begin annually on the Sunday preceding Juliette Low's birthday. The first Girl Scout *Blue Book of Rules* was published in the sixth year of the life of Girl Scouts.

By 1920, there were almost 100 Girl Scout Councils in 11 states with almost 70,000 members in over 3,000 troops. This was Juliette Low's last year as president, and she was given the title of Founder, and her birthday became Founder's Day. In this year the first International Conference of Girl Guides and Girl Scouts was held in England, and the American song, "Taps" became part of the Girl Guides and Girl Scout movements. A new handbook, *Scouting for Girls,* was published, and the monthly magazine, "The Rally" adopted a new moniker, "American Girl." A national training center, Camp Edith Macy, was opened in Briar Cliff Manor, New York.

The *Ladies' Home Journal* ran an advertisement in the April 7, 1921 issue showing Girl Scouts preparing a meal, "After the Hike." The October 22, 1921 issue of *The Literary Digest* had a Norman Rockwell cover showing a Girl Scout in khaki uniform, "One of Uncle Sam's Assets: A Girl Scout." The first national Girl Scout camp, Camp Andree Clark, was established in 1922 next to Camp Edith Macy. The Girl Scouts began publishing "Field News," a monthly newsletter for leaders, changing the name in the second year to "The Girl Scout Leader." Formal training was instituted for leaders, and two rows of seven stars and seven stripes were added to the design of the Girl Scout pin. Babe Ruth posed for a publicity photo with a Girl Scout during the "Million Cookies Drive."

The October 25, 1924 cover of The Saturday Evening Post shows a Girl Scout in green uniform, bandaging a puppy's leg. Courtesy Lynne Armstrong.

The fledgling organization continued to generate public support through media exposure. The October 25, 1924, *Saturday Evening Post* had the "Girl Scout Plays Vet" cover by Joseph C. Leyendecker that pictures

The October 22, 1921 Literary Digest by Norman Rockwell pictures a Girl Scout in khaki uniform. Courtesy Lynne Armstrong.

*The November 6, 1924 Life magazine "Good Scouts"
cover by Norman Rockwell portrays a Girl Scout in
khaki uniform. Courtesy Lynne Armstrong.*

*September 1929 Pictorial Review shows a Girl Scout
with the green camp type uniform with hat and long-
sleeved dress, holding a dog.*

a Girl Scout bandaging a dog's paw. *Life* magazine on
its November 6th cover published Norman Rockwell's,
"Good Scouts." The International Conference of Girl
Guides and Girl Scouts was held in England in 1925,
and the next year an International Conference was held
at Camp Edith Macy as the program welcomed Brownie Girl Scouts, ages seven to nine years. The *Brownie
Book for Brown Owls* was published as the first official
leader's guide for Brownies.

In 1927, representatives of U.S. Girl Scouts
attended their first international event in Switzerland, and Girl Scouts lost their founder, Juliette
Gordon Low. A World Friendship Fund was established in her memory to promote international
understanding. A new Girl Scout handbook was published, and the first United States Girl Scout troops
outside the country were registered. Thinking Day
was added to Girl Scouts' calendars for celebration
on February 22 that year.

*August 1932 Parents' Magazine cover features
an Art Deco style Girl Scout.*

The World Association of Girl Guides and Girl Scouts (WAGGGS) was formed in 1928 by the International Council, and by 1929 there were over 200,000 Girl Scouts. The September 1929 *Pictorial Review* magazine featured a cover of a Girl Scout holding a dog. In 1930, a World Flag design was adopted, and the first all-Indian Girl Scout troop was instituted at the Indian Boarding School in Pawnee, Oklahoma. The July *Good Housekeeping* magazine used an advertisement for Great Bond Bread showing a Girl Scout and a Boy Scout helping their mother fix lunch.

In 1932, March 12th was designated as the official birthday of Girl Scouts. Mrs. Helen Storrow gave Our Chalet in Adelboden, Switzerland, to the Girl Scouts. In July, Frank Dennison illustrated the cover of *The Country Gentleman* with a picture of seven Girl Scouts climbing over rocks to look at the bay. One of the most stylish magazine covers of the year was the August *Parents' Magazine* Art deco Girl Scout cover.

This picture of two Girl Scouts looking at spring buds by Jessie Wilcox Smith was on the cover of the March 1933 Good Housekeeping magazine.

The March 1933 *Good Housekeeping* cover by Jessie Wilcox Smith shows two Girl Scouts in green uniforms looking through a magnifying glass at spring buds, and this year the Girl Scout handbook was first available in Braille and large type. In 1934, the Girl Scouts launched the Mariner Scout program. *Literary Digest's* April 21st cover shows a photo of two Girl Scouts in white middy blouse and bloomer outfits with fishing poles and fish. In 1935, the first documented council-wide cookie sale of commercially baked cookies was held in Philadelphia. This was also the year the Girl Scouts expanded their program to include older girls, 14 to 17 years of age.

The 25th anniversary of Girl Scouts in the U.S. was marked in 1937, a special 25th Anniversary poster was offered in the Girl Scout catalog, and the National and International Silver Jubilee encampment was held at Camp Andree Clark with 100 girls from the United States and 26 other countries attending. The Anniversary poster was used for the cover of the *Christian Herald* July issue. In 1938, Girl Scout membership reached 500,000, and the Girl Scouts had three age levels, Brownies for ages seven to ten; Intermediate for girls ten to fourteen; and Seniors for girls fourteen to seventeen. Over one million boxes of Girl Scout cookies were sold.

At the World's Fair in New York in 1939, the Girl Scout Chalet, a miniature copy of the Swiss Our Chalet, opened as headquarters for Girl Scouts and their friends attending the Fair. Girl Scout equipment was displayed and sold there also. Our Ark opened in London, England, and over two million boxes of GS cookies were sold. The Curved Bar award was introduced in 1940 and used until 1963.

In 1941 the Wing Scout program focusing on transportation was developed for Seniors. The first Girl Scout Calendar was produced for council fundraisers in 1943, and the slogan "A million or more by 44" was used in the annual recruitment program. In 1944, a Girl Scout check for 15,430,000 hours of service was presented to President Franklin Roosevelt. A Senior Planning Conference was held at Camp Edith Macy, and the million member mark was attained. The Merchant Marines launched a Liberty ship, *S.S. Juliette Low* and more than 250,000 girls attended Girl Scout Camps.

In 1945, the Lou Henry Hoover Memorial Forest was dedicated, and in 1946 the World Badge was adopted at the 11th World Conference in France. In 1947, the organization officially became the Girl Scouts of the United States of America. The U.S. Postal Service issued a three-cent stamp in 1948 to commemorate Juliette Low; three-quarters of a million stamps were sold in her native Savannah on the first day of issue. A new design of the World Badge was adopted at the 12th World Conference in Cooperstown, New York.

The WAGGGS Pin was introduced in 1949, and membership climbed to almost 1.5 million. Girl Scouts USA was incorporated, and in 1951, the first Brownie Girl Scout Handbook for girls was published. Official motto for the newly incorporated group became "Be Prepared."

In 1952, the National Girl Scout Camping Center was dedicated in Rockwood, Maryland. In 1953 Girl Scouts USA purchased the Juliette Low birthplace in Savannah, and the site of Our Cabaña was acquired by the World Association of Girl Guides and Girl Scouts. The Annual Girl Scout week celebration date was changed in 1954 from October to March, and the Juliette Gordon Low birthplace was dedicated on October 16. The Senior Girl Roundup was held in 1956 in Michigan with 5,000 girls attending.

By 1957, there were over 3 million Girls Scouts, and the first world center for Girl Guides and Girl Scouts in the Western Hemisphere, Our Cabana, was officially opened in Cuernavaca, Mexico. The Girl Scout headquarters in New York City was dedicated, and Our Ark moved to Earls Court in London. Girl Scouts USA celebrated the Juliette Low Centennial in 1960.

Girl Scouts USA celebrated their 50th anniversary in 1962 and developed the Girl Scout Rose and Brownie Girl Scout Marigold to honor Girl Scouts. The U.S. Postal Service issued a four-cent commemorative Girl Scout stamp, and the third Senior Girl Scout Roundup was held in Vermont.

In 1963, the Intermediate age group was divided into two levels, Juniors, ages nine to eleven, and Cadettes, ages twelve to fourteen, making four groups for girls ages seven through seventeen. New handbooks and leaders' guides accompanied the new

The 1917 Girl Scout book was "Handbook for Girl Scouts." The original price was 30 cents. It has a linen type cover and wartime paper which is very poor quality and easily torn. The inside reads "How Girls Can Help Their Country/adapted from/Agnes Baden-Powell/and/Sir Robert Baden Powell's/Handbook." It is 4¾" wide x 6¾" long and was printed in Savannah, Georgia. The spine of the book reads "How Girls Can Help Their Country." Juliette Low copyrighted the book in 1917. One of the pictures shows a Girl Scout helping with ironing using a flat iron. Price today ranges from $100.00 to $250.00.

age divisions. The new Junior program included the Sign of the Arrow and the Sign of the Star. Our Ark was renamed Olave House in honor of Lord Baden-Powell's wife, Olave.

In 1964, the first Reader's Digest Foundation Grants funded Senior Girl Scout troops' community service projects. The Girl Scout handbook was published in Braille, and in 1965, the Brownie handbook was published in Spanish. Sangam, the fourth World Center, opened in Poona, India, in 1966.

The Campus Girl Scouts became an official part of the Girl Scouts USA in 1968, and the National Center West in the Bighorn Mountains of Wyoming was established. The Girl Scouts launched Eco Action in 1969, a nationwide environmental education and improvement project. By 1970, the 30 millionth member of Girl Scouts USA was registered. In 1972, the wording of the Girl Scout Promise and Law was changed and eight new Cadette Challenges were introduced.

The Girl Scouts presented a portrait of Juliette Low in 1973 to the National Portrait Gallery in Washington, D. C. The age for Brownie membership was lowered to include six-year-old girls. A bust of Juliette Low was placed in Georgia's Hall of Fame in 1974, and the Girl Scouts sold over 123 million boxes of cookies in 1975. In 1976, 150 Girl Scout delegates, ages fourteen to seventeen, attended the National Convention. The Edith Macy National Center celebrated its 50th anniversary.

The *Worlds to Explore: Handbook for Brownie and Junior Girl Scouts* was published in 1977. The Five Worlds of Interest in Girl Scouting were introduced along with the Junior Aide patch and Brownie B's Bridge to Juniors. In 1978, a stylized trefoil using three girls' silhouette profiles became the official emblem. A career exploration project for Cadette and Senior Girl Scouts, *From Dreams to Reality,* was published, and Girl Scouts began preparations to celebrate the United Nation's "Year of the Child."

In 1979, Juliette Low was inducted into the National Women's Hall of Fame in Seneca Falls, New York, and the Girl Scouts ceased publication of *American Girl.* In 1980 the Silver Award and the Gold Award became the top two awards in Cadette and Senior Girl Scouts. The Sign of the Rainbow, Sign of the Star, Sign of the Satellite, and Bridge to Cadettes were introduced into the Junior Girl Scout program.

The Girl Scouts celebrated their 70th anniversary in 1982; the Edith Macy Conference Center in New York was dedicated, and April 22 was selected as Girl Scout Leader Day. From this time, adults could now obtain lifetime memberships in the Girl Scouts.

In 1983 the Juliette Gordon Low Federal Complex, only the second such complex named after a woman, opened in Savannah. In 1984, the Girl Scouts launched a program for Daisy Girl Scouts for kindergarten age girls. The wording of the Girl Scout Promise was changed, and in 1985, the Girl Scouts introduced a contemporary issue resource, "Tune Into Well-Being, Say No to Drugs."

In 1986, Brownie Girl Scout Try-Its were introduced and to respond to changing times, Girl Scouts issued another resource, "Staying Safe, Preventing Child Abuse." The Sign of the World was introduced into the Junior program. In 1987 the Girls Scouts celebrated their 75th anniversary with the theme "Tradition with a Future." The U.S. Postal Service issued another stamp to commemorate the Girl Scouts USA.

The National Historic Preservation Center opened at the National Headquarters in New York in 1989, and in 1991, Earth Education programs were introduced. In 1996, new wording for the Girl Scout law was adopted, and separate handbooks for Cadettes and Seniors were published. In 1997, the Girl Scouts celebrated 85 years and from all over the United States, girls met on the mall in Washington, D.C. to sing songs. Cadettes and Seniors were urged to participate in community service and career exploration. The Girl Scouts remains, in 2002, the largest volunteer organization for girls in the world.

Juliette Gordon Low died on January 17, 1927. She was buried wearing her Girl Scout uniform with her decoration of honor, the jeweled Thanks Badge of the Girl Scout, and the Silver Fish of the Girl Guides. In her uniform pocket was a folded telegram that read: "You are not only the first Girl Scout, you are the best Girl Scout of them all." She changed the lives of millions of girls with the revolutionary idea that girls could do anything.

"Girl Scout₄ Vignettes" © 1999 Merana Cadorette all rights reserved

This wonderful Merana Cadorette watercolor, "Girl Scout Vignettes," shows a chronology of mini-scenes of various Girl Scout activities, badges, costumes, and symbols. Original watercolor by Merana Cadorette, ©1999; www.merana.com, P.O. Box 690445, Vero Beach, FL, 32969-0445.

Earliest Girl Scout Dolls

The earliest Girl Scout doll reported is a 6½" composition one. She retains her original box dated July 13, 1917, but there are no tags or manufacturer's name. This earliest Girl Scout is all original with blond mohair wig, painted side-glancing eyes, rosy cheeks, smiling closed mouth, brown eyebrows, and a brown gabardine dress with matching scarf and hat. The dress is accented with dark brown thread decorating the hem, belt, cuffs, and scarf.

Her hands are composition, somewhat out of proportion to the rest of her body with the fingers molded together. She has molded and painted black legs and feet to appear as black boots. She was purchased at auction.

Dolls of this era were made from many different formulas of composition, and some of the production methods were more successful than others. This doll does not appear to have been constantly played-with, noting her rosy cheek color and intact costume. However, her composition finish has cracked, and some paint is missing from her boots.

Early 6½" composition Girl Scout has side-glancing, painted black flirty eyes showing white highlights, light brown eyebrows, rosy cheeks, closed smiling mouth, blond mohair wig, composition arms, and legs and feet painted black to resemble boots. This doll was likely not officially authorized by the Girl Scouts. $250.00. Courtesy Lynne Armstrong.

Girl Scout Dolls 1920s – 1930s

Leather, circa 1920s – 1930s

5" one-piece leather Girl Scout doll with printed features and clothing has a dark green shirt and bloomers, and khaki hat representing the style worn in the 1920s and 1930s. She has a red neck scarf tied in the early way. This novelty item by an unknown manufacturer has a string sewn inside; doll is not official. $100.00.

Printed Cloth

Newspapers and magazines advertised these dolls. With the basic doll printed, these simple dolls allowed the maker to embellish them with embroidery, stuff with cotton, then stitch together. One example shows a Girl Scout dressed in a 1920s camp uniform with cap, embroidered red tie, white blouse, and brown bloomers, with her hand raised in salute.

The first official Girl Scout doll was found in the fall of 1920 in *American Girl*, a magazine for Girl Scouts, and the doll was offered for sale until March 1922 when it was discontinued. The cost of the doll was $2.00.

If the doll pictured on page 18 is compared with the picture on page 198 of the *Girl Scout Collector's Guide*, one can see the similarity. This doll remains with the original owner, brought to her by a friend of her parents in 1929 as a gift. The mold of Little Sister was used, and she is marked on the shoulder "Grace Corry." The body is stamped "Genuine Madame Hendren Doll//made in USA."

13½" stuffed all-cloth Girl Scout with flat face, has embroidered features including hair, side-glancing eyes, eyebrows, nostrils, and mouth. She wears a 1920s camp uniform with white shirt, red scarf, brown cap, and bloomers. This is an unofficial doll. $65.00.

Front and back of printed 13½" cloth doll on page 16, showing embroidered details.

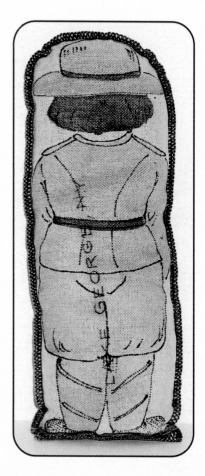

Front and back views of 8" printed cloth doll stuffed with wood shavings which was sold as a World War I dough-boy. With the long hair and more feminine face, it more closely resembles a 1920s Girl Scout camp uniform. She wears a brown uniform with jacket, belt, bloomers, hat, and matching leggings. The shirt has two pockets and four buttons down the front. Marked on the back is "Lake George, NY." This is an unofficial doll. $25.00.

Madame Georgene Averill, Paul Averill, Georgene Novelties, circa 1927 – 1929

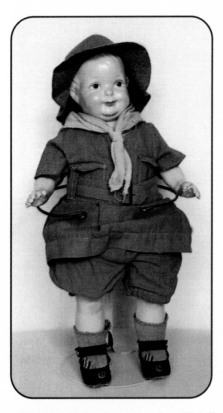

13" composition Georgene Averill doll designed by Grace Corry, with cloth body; her arms and legs are composition. Painted features, molded painted hair and brows, and closed mouth. She wears a two-piece brown khaki camp uniform with a long blouse with two upper pockets, brown fabric belt with buckle, bloomers, and brown felt hat. The shoes are black, socks are brown, and the tie is yellow. It is not known for sure if the doll is official. $350.00 – 700.00. Photo courtesy Pidd Miller.

Averill operated under several names; the first was Averill Manufacturing Company, circa 1915 – 1930s; Paul Averill 1920 – 1924; Madame Georgene 1920 – 1927; and Georgene Novelties 1920 – 1940s. Georgene Hopf married Paul Averill; their family business included their daughter and several of Georgene's brothers. Paul handled the business part of the manufacturing business, and Georgene was the creative partner. She was also called Madame Hendren, which became their trademark name, and she is best known for her design of the Mama doll using a cloth body with a crier inserted. Averill made composition dolls with the earliest dolls dressed as Dutch children and Indians in felt costumes. Georgene also designed the bisque "Bonnie Babe," as well as a large line of composition dolls. In addition, the Averill Company made many cloth dolls such as Raggedy Ann and Andy and later also the Girl Scout and Brownie Dolls. Georgene Novelties made official Girl Scout and Brownie dolls in the 1930s through 1957.

Grace Corry, born 1897 in Oklahoma Indian Territory, moved as an adult to Alabama, first studying to become a teacher and then studying art in New York City. She experimented painting cloth dolls. She patented her first doll in 1920, a cloth "Fiji-Wiji" with painted features. She sculpted "Little Brother" and "Little Sister" in 1927 for Averill Manufacturing Company and was pleased with her work's presentation as produced by Averill. She married Sidney J. Rockwell who worked for *Playthings*, the trade magazine of the toy industry. Grace Corry Rockwell died in 1973.

Khaki Uniform Dolls, circa 1920s

There are several known examples of dolls in khaki uniforms, but none of these examples is official. These were dolls dressed in homemade uniforms, and it is too bad we do not know their stories. The first example on page 19 is 26" tall and in full uniform with bloomers. Mold number 250, patented by the German firm of Ernst Heubach in 1914, she is described as having a character face with sleep eyes and an open mouth with teeth. Her head is made of bisque with a composition and wood ball-jointed body. She wears German-made shoes and cotton socks. The maker of this costume is unknown.

Starting in 1920, the Girl Scout crests on the left bodice were embroidered with a black border. In 1922, chevrons on her left sleeve were embroidered with cotton thread. The chevrons denote the rank held in the troop, and in the example shown, the two chevrons mean patrol leader. On the inside of this doll's dress is a trademark imprint in a 2" circle with the Girl Scout National Headquarters address of "189 Lexington Avenue, New York City." This was the address of the national headquarters until 1924 when it moved to 670 Lexington Avenue. This doll and the outfit date to the 1922 – 1924 time period.

The outfit is wonderfully made with French seams. Girl Scout buttons were used on the front of the skirt, skirt waistband, bloomer waistband, and bottom of bloomers. The red tie is cut down from an original one and is tied correctly in a tie knot rather than the square knot we associate with the 1950s.

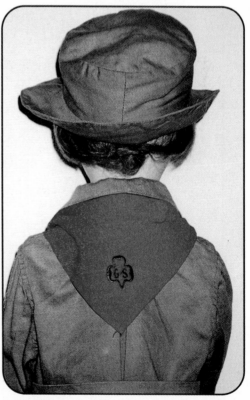

26" bisque Ernst Heubach mold 250, brown mohair wig, sleep eyes, multi-stroke painted brown brows, red accent marks at inner eye, open mouth with teeth, and dimple in chin, wearing 1922 to 1924 Girl Scout full uniform with bloomers, $900.00.

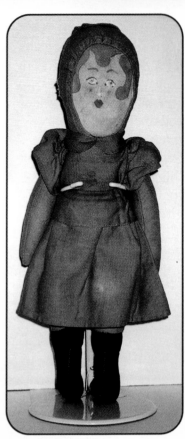

10" composition unmarked Patsy-type doll with molded and painted hair, blue painted side-glancing eyes, and closed mouth wears a 1919 – 1927 style homesewn two-piece khaki Girl Scout uniform with brimmed hat. Uniform is made of original Girl Scout cloth with embroidered badges, troop crest, and GS on collar tips. Outfit only, $175.00. *Courtesy Lynne Armstrong.*

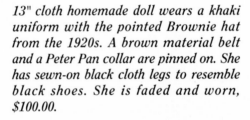

13" cloth homemade doll wears a khaki uniform with the pointed Brownie hat from the 1920s. A brown material belt and a Peter Pan collar are pinned on. She has sewn-on black cloth legs to resemble black shoes. She is faded and worn, $100.00.

Another example of doll dressed in a homemade 1920s khaki camp uniform is this 15" composition doll from a later era, marked on back of neck "Made in USA/PAT No. 2252077," a shoulderhead, with full composition arms, and composition legs to knees, and a cloth mama doll body with working crier. The official GS material is marked inside "GS (inside of trefoil)/ 670 Lexington Avenue, New York City" which dates the material from 1924 to 1928. A convention in October 1927 adopted a new green material for the Girl Scouts. This outfit has a brown long-sleeved shirt, belt, and bloomers. Her matching brown hat has a brim. She wears a bright yellow rayon tie and black socks. This costume would not be considered official. $300.00. *Photo courtesy Pauline Baker.*

Converse Flexy, circa 1925 – 1929

In 1929, a wooden flexy doll was shown in the Girl Scout National Equipment Catalog. The ad reads, "a jointed wooden Flexy Doll. Suitable for G. S. window displays when dressed 'in uniform'. Also for hospitals and Christmas trees. K – 901 $0.15". This doll may have been available as early as 1925. The Flexy Doll was designed by Helen Sargent Hitchcock (distantly related to artist John Singer Sargent). "She folds, she floats and she's flexible and funny." It was painted by Lucille Patterson Marsh and made by Converse of Winchendon, Massachusetts. Some dolls are marked on the back "Flexy Doll," but most now have the printing worn off. These are hard to find since they break easily. An official doll, this doll is made of ¼" pressed wood and is 9" tall.

 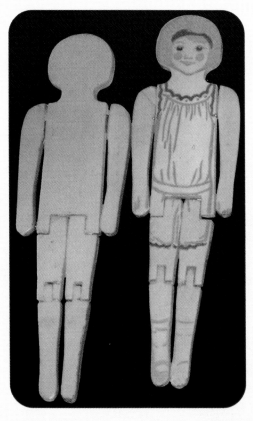

9" pressed wood Converse "Flexy Doll" with painted features, undergarments, and shoes. She has jointed arms, hips, and knees and is marked on the back "Flexy Doll." The dress has a matching belt and hat with a red scarf, circa 1925 – 1929; $75.00 – $250.00.

Albert Schoenhut and Co., 1913 – 1926, 1935, Philadelphia, Pennsylvania

Albert Schoenhut made multi-jointed spring wooden dolls with painted features from 1911 to the mid-1930s. They were wonderfully versatile play dolls that could be posed in many different positions. Children as well as babies and toddlers were produced with molded or painted hair or wigs. The dolls had holes in their feet and came with a metal stand with a prong that would fit into the foot, allowing the doll to stand on one leg.

The Schoenhut Company made "Pinn Dolls" for a short time, starting with a copyright date of 1935. The Pinn Doll was designed by Emily T. Myers in September of 1935 and produced by one of the sons of the original founder, Otto Schoenhut, along with Stanley Osborn and his nephew George Weber Schoenhut. These were manufactured in the vacant warehouse that once housed the family business. The Pinn Doll is an all-wooden jointed doll with flat painted face and yarn hair. The clothing is tacked on.

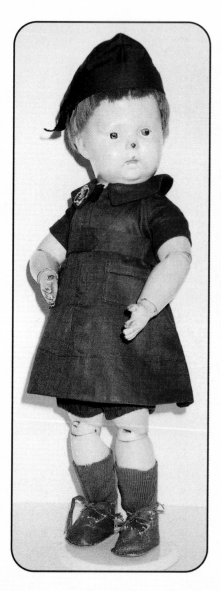

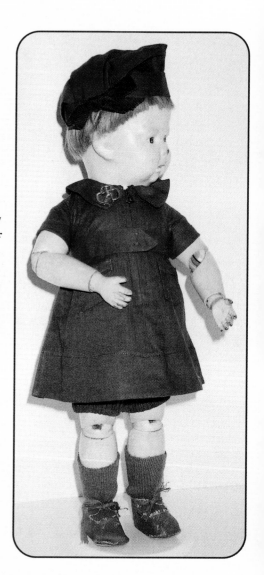

16" wooden Schoenhut model 108 W toddler doll is wearing an unmarked uniform that might be factory made or constructed by an excellent seamstress. The style of costume represents a Brownie from the late 1920s to the 1930s. Schoenhut made this model doll from 1913 – 1926. Her hat is the peaked style that lies down to one side. The brown cotton dress has matching belt and bloomers. The material seems to be the type used during this time for Brownie uniforms. She has brown oilcloth shoes and cotton socks. This is not an official licensed doll. Costume, $75.00; doll, $450.00.

12" wooden Schoenhut Pinn Doll dressed as a Girl Scout. She has yellow yarn hair and painted features with side-glancing wyes. Her uniform is made of green cotton, and she wears a darker green felt hat. Her paper tag reads: "CLO//PINN," and she is marked on the bottom of the foot, "Patent Pending//1935//E.T.M. St. Paul Minn." This doll is not official, $250.00. Courtesy Pidd Miller.

Retired pediatrician Dr. Pidd Miller shown with her husband, Alfred W. Kobs, holds a wooden Schoenhut Clo Pinn doll. Pidd Miller is a lifelong Girl Scout enthusiast and developed the Girl Scout Doll Collecting Patch with the San Jacinto Girl Scout Council in Houston, Texas. The Texas State Legislature and the San Jacinto Girl Scout Council have both named Miller one of the "Women of Distinction." Pidd Miller was a member of the first Brownie troop in Houston formed in 1929; her mother was the troop leader and later Pidd was leader for her daughter's Brownie and Girl Scout troops. Pidd Miller received the Award of Excellence for her work with Girl Scouts from the United Federation of Doll clubs. In addition, Miller organized, in 1997, a "Dolly goes to College" held at Houston Baptist University that allows Girl Scouts and their dolls to tour the college and meet faculty and students. Miller also created a "Share a Doll" service project in 1995.

For more information regarding the Girl Scout Doll Collecting Patch, send a S.A.S.E. to: Pidd Miller, P.O. Box 631092 Houston, TX, 77263 – 1092

Effanbee Doll Company, 1928 – 1939

Bernard E. Fleischaker and Hugo Baum began manufacturing dolls in 1913. They combined the initials from their names to name the new company "Effanbee." This company has survived wars, recessions, and numerous changes of ownership and is still viable today. In the early years they made dolls from composition, a glue-based product with fillers of wood pulp and other materials. The early dolls had composition heads and hands and cloth bodies sometimes stuffed with sawdust or straw.

They produced a line of all-composition dolls in the late 1920s and during the 1930s, and one of their top sellers was renamed "Patsy" in January of 1928 after initially being introduced as "Mimi" in December of 1927. Because there were copyright infringements on the name of "Mimi," the ever-adaptable Effanbee pulled the name of Patsy from earlier "Mama" dolls made with cloth bodies and criers.

Patsy was revolutionary at the time because of her patented neck joint that allowed the doll to be attached to a composition five-piece body. Patsy was a 13½" doll with red painted hair, headband, painted side-glancing eyes, and closed painted mouth. In 1929, Effanbee added a 19" Patsy Ann as her older sister, followed by a whole bevy of other family members. Patsy was one of the first dolls to have other companies manufacture wardrobes and accessories for her. They made shoes, roller skates, raincoats, beach pajamas, swimsuits, dresses, coats, hats, and sleepwear as well as such remarkable things as celluloid eyeglasses. "Glad Togs" and "Dolly Togs" were brand names of companies that made copies of Girl Scout uniforms to fit the Patsy family of dolls as well as for other dolls in the early to mid-1930s.

Glad Togs was the trademark of Gladys G. Myers of Seattle, Washington. Dolly Togs were made in Melrose, Massachusetts. In 1928, the material for the Girl Scout uniform changed

19" composition Effanbee Patsy Ann, circa 1929+, wears a factory-made Girl Scout uniform tagged "DOLLY TOGS//MELROSE, MASS." An added item is a small metal bugle attached to her belt. Her tie is made of silk-like material. She wears green socks and cream side-snap leatherette shoes with silver metal buckle. Patsy Ann has molded/painted red bobbed hair with bangs, sleep eyes, closed pouty mouth, and five-piece composition body, $900.00.

This advertisement for Glad Togs appeared in the toy trade publication Toy World in June of 1932 and ran in each issue until the end of the year.

to a gray-green color and examples from Glad Togs and Dolly Togs have been found. With no mention of these costumes being sanctioned by the Girl Scouts, they are termed not to be official. However, the costumes would be termed "original" as they were commercially made for these dolls, were made in the same era as the dolls, and would be correct if you were entering the doll in competition.

19" composition Effanbee Patsy Ann, circa 1929+, wears a tagged "GLAD TOGS" Girl Scout uniform made from the official Girl Scout material at this time. She has an older Girl Scout pin on her hat. Her side-snap shoes are made of black leatherette, and she has a yellow cotton tie. $600.00. Photo courtesy Diane Miller.

19" composition Effanbee Patsy Ann, circa 1929+, wears a factory made Girl Scout uniform tagged "DOLLY TOGS//MELROSE, MASS." Patsy Ann shoes are replaced. The Patsy Ann doll was introduced in 1929 and sold throughout the 1930s. $900.00.

17" Effanbee composition "Betty Brite" with green sleep eyes on marked Patsy Joan body wears a homemade Brownie outfit. This is a copy of the first Brownie oufit, circa 1928, and has the peaked hat, lace front brown cotton dress with fabric belt, long brown stockings, and old lace-up saddle oxford shoes. She wears matching brown cotton bloomers. Doll only, circa 1932, $125.00; early costume by Mary Eskridge, priceless.

15" unmarked composition Patsy-type doll wears a factory-made Girl Scout uniform tagged, "DOLLY TOGS//MEDFORD, MASS." She has a green silk ribbon tie. While Dolly Togs used official Girl Scout material, no mention has been found of the doll being sanctioned by the Girl Scouts. Not official, $400.00.

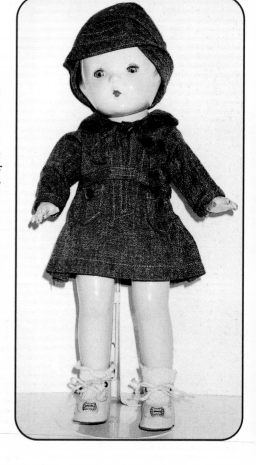

13½" composition Effanbee Patsy with molded red hair with headband, painted khaki colored side-glancing eyes with white highlights, painted eyebrows, closed pouty mouth, and five-piece composition body with bent right arm. This doll wears her metal heart bracelet that reads "EFFANBEE DURABLE DOLLS." She wears the gray-green Girl Scout uniform tagged "DOLLY TOGS," but the belt is missing. Not official, $500.00. Photo courtesy Lynne Armstrong.

Alexander Doll Company, 1935

An article in the July 1935 *American Girl* magazine highlights "Little People on Strings," marionettes by Tony Sarg, a master of marionettes. Sarg explains how to make a marionette and how to control them. The Girl Scout marionette is marked "Madame Alexander//Tony Sarg." This doll is probably not official.

12" composition Alexander Doll Company Tony Sarg marionette is dressed in the gray-green handmade Scout uniform with green felt hat. The doll has painted features, human hair wig, and small holes in hands to attach strings. The head, hands, and legs are composition with molded painted black shoes. She is marked "Madame Alexander//Tony Sarg." $400.00.

16" unmarked composition Shirley Temple look-alike doll with wig, open mouth and teeth, and sleep eyes wears a home-made Girl Scout uniform with matching belt and a maroon silk tie. The doll and uniform may be from the late 1930s. This is not an official doll. Uniform, $50.00; doll $75.00.

16" unmarked composition Patsy-type doll wears a handmade uniform of green cotton with gold "G.S." embroidered on the collar. This costume would date from the 1930s and is not official, $250.00.

Singer Sewing Machine Company, 1935

In the November 1935 issue of *American Girl*, there is a Singer Sewing Machine Company ad which shows a dressed Girl Scout doll and urges, "DRESS A GIRL SCOUT DOLL!" Singer claims that it "will help you make good Scouts out of old dolls" and states, "Dig up a doll and bring it down to Singer. We will help you draft a pattern and show you exactly how to make a miniature copy of your own smart uniform…hat, dress, tie, socks and shoes." The magazine also gives directions for making the costume in an article "Dressing a Girl Scout Doll" by Elizabeth Anthony. The doll pictured with the pattern is all-cloth, 14" tall, and beautifully made with a handpainted face with blue side-glancing eyes. She is wearing the camp uniform consisting of a shirt, tie, and bloomers. She wears commercially-made black leatherette shoes that tie and have a metal buckle on the toe. Singer also gives directions for a long dress and a hat with a brim. Since the directions are presented in the Girl Scout publication, it is assumed the costume is official.

14" all-cloth doll dressed in 1935 Girl Scout camp uniform from American Girl magazine, the official publication of the Girl Scouts. The uniform is green with button-closing belt and red tie. The doll has a black wig, painted features, and cloth hands with stitched fingers. $400.00. Photos courtesy Pidd Miller.

Georgene Novelties, 1936 – 1939

Georgene Averill of Georgene Novelties made Girl Scout and Brownie dolls for 20 years, 1936 to 1956. In 1936, the Girl Scout National Equipment Catalog shows an all-cloth Georgene Novelties Brownie doll with a pointed hat. The hands are mitt style with defined thumbs. Brown sewn-on fabric represents brown shoes. She has printed bangs with an overlay of paint and painted brown eyes with white highlights on her flat face. Her yarn braids are attached on either side below the painted hair. The dress with matching panties is made from official cotton cloth. The dress has a Peter Pan collar, and the material belt is pinned on. The hat is a triangle and is laid over and pinned on the head's right side. There are two pockets on the skirt. The top of the dress is pinned together. Pictured with matching Girl Scout cookie cardboard can with metal top and bottom from the same era, this is an official doll.

The 1937 Girl Scout catalog shows a new Brownie doll with a new face. The face is flat, larger, and rounder than the 1936 doll. She is 14" tall, with large painted blue eyes with white highlights. She has painted lashes and brows and a closed painted mouth. She is wearing a brown cotton uniform made from official material which features the Peter Pan collar and pointed hat. Her belt is pinned on, and the hat has a stud holding it down on the right side of the head. Her hair and bangs are yellow yarn. This doll is official.

16" all-cloth official Georgene Novelties Brownie doll with brown painted side-glancing eyes, printed bangs overlaid with paint, yellow yarn pigtails, mitt hands, sewn-on shoes, dressed in original Brownie uniform with pointed hat, shown with a Girl Scout cardboard cookie can with metal top and bottom. Mint doll, $400.00; can, $85.00.
Mint doll, courtesy Diane Miller.

16" all-cloth official Georgene Novelties Brownie doll with brown painted side-glancing eyes, printed bangs overlaid with paint, yellow yarn pigtails, mitt hands, sewn-on shoes, dressed in original Brownie uniform with pointed hat, well played-with, $100.00.

14" all-cloth Georgene Novelties official Brownie with flat face, painted blue eyes, painted lashes, brows, and mouth. The all-cloth body has mitt hands with defined thumbs and sewn-on brown cloth shoes. She wears a brown cotton dress with Peter Pan collar and matching belt. She has the pointed Brownie hat. $400.00.

1940s – 1950s, The Most Prolific Era

Georgene Novelties, 1940 – 1957

14" all-cloth Georgene Novelties official Brownie with flat face, painted blue eyes, painted lashes, brows, and mouth. The all-cloth body has mitt hands with defined thumbs and sewn-on brown cloth shoes. She wears a brown cotton dress with Peter Pan collar and matching belt. She has the pointed Brownie hat. $400.00.

14" all-cloth Georgene Novelties official Girl Scout "Sylvia" with yellow yarn hair, painted blue eyes, and closed painted mouth. She has mitt style hands with defined thumb and sewn-on brown cloth shoes. She wears a green belted uniform with red tie. The hat is dark green felt with a white painted Girl Scout emblem, $400.00.

The 1940 Girl Scout catalog had two Georgene Novelties dolls, "Official dolls in official uniforms stand 14" high. Bangs, curls and plaits are of mercerized yarn, and uniforms are removable so Brownie and Sylvia can be dressed in the national costume or Girl Scout uniform of other nations. 11 – 941 Brownie, $1.25. 11 – 942 Sylvia, $1.50."

The first Girl Scout doll wears a green one-piece dress with matching panties, she wears a red tie, and her belt is pinned on. Her hat is darker green felt with the Girl Scout emblem painted on. The first Brownie was named Sylvia and is shown with the pointed hat. Sylvia has a flat face with painted blue eyes, yellow yarn braids, mitt hands with defined thumbs, and sewn-on brown cloth shoes.

Compare the 1940 Georgene pair (top) with the 14" all-cloth Georgene Novelties 1942 official Brownie. The dress style no longer has the Peter Pan rounded collar, instead has a pointed shirt collar. The pointed elf-type hat has been changed to a six-gore beanie style. The eyes now are painted with a side-glancing look on both the Brownie and the Girl Scout. Each, $400.00.

The 1942 Girl Scout catalog shows Sylvia and a Brownie priced at $1.75 each. The order number for the Brownie was 11-943, and she had red yarn braids. The style and material for the Brownie uniform have also changed. The hat is no longer the pointed elf-type hat, but now is the six-gore beanie with a Brownie on it. The Brownie uniform no longer has a Peter Pan collar but now has a pointed shirt collar. Both dresses are one piece with pinned-on belts. The buttons are decorative, and the dress is fastened with a straight pin.

Sometime during the war years of 1941 – 1944, the Brownie material was changed to a brown cotton pin-checked gingham for the uniforms for both Brownie girls and Brownie dolls. These dolls are very hard to find, and this author has seen only two of them.

14" all-cloth Georgene Novelties official Brownie doll, circa 1941 – 1944, with painted features, side-glancing painted blue eyes, painted lashes and brows, painted closed mouth, red yarn bangs and pigtails. She retains her cloth body with mitt hands and defined thumbs. Her shoes are dark brown sewn-on cloth. The pins checked ginghamdress has the pointed shirt collar, buttons on the front, and a matching belt, $450.00.

Advertisement for Georgene Novelties, Inc. dolls from the Toys and Novelties trade publication, August 1935.

Full-length view of 14" all-cloth Georgene Novelties official Brownie.

In 1946 came another change in the design of the Georgene Novelties Girl Scout dolls. Now 13" tall, the face has gone from the flat to a molded mask face. The doll's uniform color has changed to a brighter green. She still comes with matching panties, and the clothes now fasten with dark green snaps. The dress is one-piece with long sleeves and cuffs, and there are two pockets on the skirt. Her belt is now made of oilcloth (leatherette) and closes with a snap. The leatherette shoes tie at the ankle and have a silver buckle on the toe. The ties for the Girl Scouts range from red to orange to gold. Girl Scouts come with blonde hair; a rare example is a black Girl Scout that was not advertised in the catalogs. These dolls were available until 1954. They are official and ranged in price from $2.95 to $3.50.

The Brownie doll also has a mask face and floss hair in either red or blonde. There is also a black version with black hair. The Brownie hat is a brown felt beanie, but there is no Brownie silhouette on the cap. The dress is a brown cotton, short-sleeved with one pocket on the upper bodice. The dress has two snap button closures, and the matching belt closes with one brown snap button. The Brownie has matching panties, and the shoes range in color from medium brown to dark brown to black. Original dolls carry a blue and silver round Georgene hangtag.

Three 14" all-cloth Georgene Novelties official Brownie dolls. The center doll is a much darker color and was thought to be an example of a black Brownie. However, further research indicates the cloth had a rubberized paint that has discolored with time. Each, $400.00.

Close up of 14" all-cloth Georgene Novelties Brownie with red yarn hair shows blue painted eyes, painted lashes and brows, closed mouth, and rosy cheeks.

Above left: 13" all-cloth Georgene Novelties official Brownie with red floss hair, mask face, painted side-glancing blue eyes, closed mouth, and mitt hands with defined thumb. She wears a short-sleeved brown cotton dress with one pocket on the upper bodice. The dress is fastened with two brown snap buttons, and the matching belt fastens with one brown snap button. She wears matching brown panties and a brown felt beanie. The redhead is hard to find with a mask face. $100.00 – 250.00.

Above right: 13" all-cloth Georgene Novelties official Girl Scout with blonde embroidery floss hair, molded mask face, painted side-glancing blue eyes, painted lashes above the eye, painted brows, red accents at the nostrils, and painted closed mouth. She wears the green long-sleeved dress with two pockets on skirt, leatherette belt, and green felt hat. She carries the silver and blue Georgene hangtag on her wrist. $250.00.

Above center and right: 13" all-cloth Georgene Novelties official Brownie with yellow floss hair, blue painted side-glancing eyes, painted lashes above the eye, and mask face, with a brown cotton short- sleeved dress with one pocket on the upper bodice, and brown snap buttons. She has a matching cotton brown belt that closes with a brown snap button. Her hat is a brown felt beanie, and her black shoes have ties at the ankle. $100.00 – 250.00.

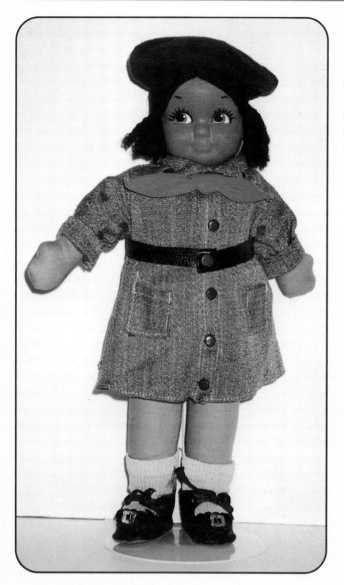

13" all-cloth Georgene Novelties official black Girl Scout with black yarn hair, mask face, brown painted side-glancing eyes, closed mouth, and mitt hands with defined thumb. She wears a long-sleeved green cotton dress with two patch pockets on the skirt. The dress is fastened with green snap buttons, and the matching belt fastens with one green snap button. She wears matching panties and a green felt hat. Her shoes are black leatherette with ankle tie. $250.00.

13" black all-cloth Georgene Novelties official Brownie with black floss hair, mask face, painted side-glancing brown eyes with white highlights, closed mouth, and mitt hands with defined thumb. She wears a short-sleeved brown cotton dress with one pocket on the upper bodice. The dress is fastened with two brown snap buttons, and the matching belt fastens with one brown snap button. She wears matching brown panties and a brown felt beanie. She carries a silver and blue Georgene hangtag. $100.00 – 250.00.

Close-up of Georgene silver and blue hangtag, reads "A//Genuine//Georgene//Doll//A Product of//Georgene Novelties, Inc.//New York//Made in U.S.A."

The 1951 Girl Scout catalog shows one of the most rare Georgene Novelties dolls to be found. In the *Girls Scouts Collector Guide,* we are told that only 500 of the Girl Scout Mariner Doll were made from 1951 to 1955. The first doll, 1951 – 1952, has a white stripe around the waist. The uniform consists of a blouse with sailor collar trimmed with white stripes, a black cotton triangle tie, a skirt with four pleats, and matching pants with white stripes on the side. The hat has four gores and is from the same material as the outfit. The second doll has the same outfit without the white stripes on the waistband. This waistband has a blue snap. The shoes are black leatherette, and the socks are white. These two dolls are all original and official.

13" all-cloth Georgene Novelties Mariner Doll with mask face, yellow floss wig with bangs, painted eyebrows, painted blue eyes with white highlights, seven painted lashes on each eye, closed slightly smiling mouth, and mitt hands with defined thumb. The 1951 – 1952 Mariner's costume is a blue sailor dress with collar with striped trim and has two white stripes around the waist. The 1953 – 1955 Mariner's costume is identical without stripes around the waist. These dolls are very rare. Each, $750.00+. Photos courtesy Bob Trowbridge.

13" all-cloth Georgene Novelties, Mariner Doll, with mask face, yellow floss wig with bangs, painted eyebrows, painted blue eyes with white highlights, seven painted lashes on each eye, closed slightly smiling mouth, and mitt hands with defined thumb. These dolls are very rare. Each, $750.00+.

The Georgene Novelties era for Girl Scout dolls ends with the 1955/1957 catalogs. The 13" dolls from this era now have vinyl heads stuffed with cotton and are marked on the back of the head "GEORGENE." This type of early vinyl may become oily to the touch, as the vinyl production was not perfected. They now have blue plastic glassine eyes with more painted lashes above the eye. Their hair is yarn, and they have cloth bodies that seem a bit slimmer. They wear the same style dresses with matching panties. Their final showing is in the 1957 Girl Scout catalog. Now rare, these official dolls originally sold for $3.50 each.

Close-up of 13" vinyl Georgene Girl Scout and Brownie with glassine eyes, painted lashes, yarn hair, and painted brows.

13" vinyl Georgene Novelties Girl Scout doll with yarn hair, blue plastic eyes, many painted lashes above the eye, painted brown eyebrows, closed mouth, and cloth body with mitt hands and defined thumb. The Scout wears the green one-piece dress with snap buttons and two pockets on the skirt, black leatherette belt with snap button closure. She has a yellow tie, a green felt (possibly replacement) hat, and brown leatherette tie shoes. $75.00 – 250.00.

13" vinyl Georgene Novelties Brownie doll with yarn hair, blue plastic eyes, painted lashes above the eye, painted brown eyebrows, closed mouth, and cloth body with mitt hands and defined thumb. She wears the brown one-piece dress with two snaps and matching belt with snap closure. The Brownie has a felt beanie hat and brown tie shoes. $75.00 – 250.00.

Terri Lee, 1946 – 1960

16" painted plastic Patent Pending Terri Lee with blonde wig, brown painted side-glancing eyes, painted upper lashes and eyebrows, closed mouth, hard plastic five-piece body. She is dressed in original Girl Scout uniform with long sleeves that button at cuffs, button-down collar, and button front closure. The dress has one pocket on the bodice, two pockets on the skirt, and a dark green "leatherette" belt. She wears a dark green felt tam hat with the Girl Scout emblem in white and has brown and white saddle oxford shoes with white socks. The dress is tagged "Terri Lee" in blue lettering on a white rayon tag; this first tag was used circa 1947 – 1950. She also has an official white paper tag with green Girl Scout emblem that reads, "Uniforms approved by/the Girl Scouts//of the United States of//America. $700.00 – 900.00.

The Terri Lee Doll Company was started by Violet Lee of Clarinda, Iowa. Violet used a likeness sculpted in 1945 by her niece Maxine Runci of her own daughter, Drienne. Maxine had the artistic talent and Violet the entrepreneurial drive to take an idea and see it through. Violet moved to Lincoln, Nebraska, and married a dentist, Dr. Harry Milton Gradwohl. They had one child named Harriet Wilma, who took the nickname of Terri Lee which the doll was also dubbed. Violet and Maxine took their doll to the annual Toy Fair in New York City where it was well received. Upon returning home, Maxine made prototype heads, and Violet started a cottage industry for assembling the composition dolls with a loan of $11,000.00 from her husband. Terri Lee was featured in the 1946 catalog, and they sold 8,000 dolls that first year. Violet took over control of the business and added workers and found new work space. Early in 1947, she experimented with various forms of plastic materials for the bodies and settled on a product call Tenite by Tennessee Eastman Company.

Violet Lee Gradwohl found an experienced manager, Grace Hast, as the business kept expanding. Grace worked for the Girl Scout organization while going to college. She also worked for the United Relief Rehabilitation Association, and these experiences led to the Terri Lee industry employing many handicapped persons. Grace was seamstress, bookkeeper, purchasing agent, office and production manager for Terri Lee. When the plant relocated from Lincoln, Nebraska to Apple Valley, California, Hast stayed with the company until 1958. After a disastrous fire and legal problems, the plant was sold in 1960. Gradwohl tried to make a comeback, but failed.

Probably the company made Girl Scout dressed Terri Lee dolls because of the influence and associations of Grace Hast. They made those uniforms from 1948 – 1958 when Terri Lee also dressed Camp Fire and Blue Bird dolls. In addition, Terri Lee also furnished Brownie and Girl Scout costumes for Cosmopolitan 8" Ginger type dolls.

In 1949, the Terri Lee Company produced official Girl Scout and Brownie dressed dolls. The painted plastic doll is 16" tall, with closed mouth and side-glancing painted eyes, and is marked "Terri Lee//Pat. Pending." Through the years, the uniforms changed very little, losing pockets and going from handsewn deep hems to machine-sewn shirttail type hems. The Brownie lost the detail on her belt and hat. There are five different Girl Scout uniforms and six different Brownie uniforms reported from that era.

The Girl Scout uniform is a green long-sleeved dress that buttons at the cuffs and down the front. It has two pockets on the skirt and a button-down collar. It has a black belt that buckles and a gold satin ribbon, and she wears brown-and-white saddle oxfords with white stockings. The hat is a dark green tam with the Girl Scout emblem and G.S. initials in white. The earliest tag on the uniform reads "Terri Lee," is blue printing on white, and dates from 1947 – 1950.

The first Terri Lee Brownie used the brown-wigged 16" painted plastic model with five-piece body that has painted side-glancing eyes, eyebrows, and closed mouth. The first uniform is a brown cotton short-sleeved dress with three front buttons and a pocket on the upper left bodice. She has a buckled belt of the same fabric. She wears brown and white oxfords and white socks and a brown felt beanie. This first dress is also tagged "Terri Lee" in blue lettering on a white rayon tag, circa 1947 – 1950. A white paper tag with green Girl Scout emblem and green lettering that states this is the approved uniform is included with each costume.

16" painted plastic Terri Lee with brunette wig, brown painted side-glancing eyes, painted lashes and eyebrows, closed mouth, and five-piece body, marked "Terri Lee//Pat. Pending." She wears a short-sleeved Brownie uniform with three buttons down the front, a same fabric belt, and one patch pocket on the bodice of her dress. She wears brown and white saddle oxfords with white socks. She also has the same first tag with "Terri Lee" in blue lettering on a white tag. Her official white paper tag with green Girl Scout emblem reads "Uniforms approved by/the Girl Scouts //of the United States of/America." $700.00 – 900.00.

White woven rayon tag with blue printed script; this was the first sewn-in label used by Terri Lee, circa 1947 – 1950.

The next variation in the Terri Lee Girl Scout uniform has a change from buttons to gripper snaps on the cuffs, collar, and down the front of the dress. Some dark green tam hats have a much smaller emblem, and some still have the larger white logo emblem. The costumes are now tagged "Terri Lee," printed on satin-type ribbon.

The final variation of Girl Scout uniform for Terri Lee dolls no longer has a pocket on the bodice, and some hems are still deep hems but some now are the smaller machine-sewn shirttail hems. A third style sewn-on dress label of white satin-type ribbon has "Terri Lee" printed in blue in larger letters.

Two 16" hard plastic Terri Lee Girl Scout dolls, one with blonde wig, the other, brunette. Both have painted brown eyes with white highlights, painted brows and lashes, and closed pouty mouths. Both costumes have gripper snap closures. The costume on the left now has a narrow machine-sewn hem and no pocket on the bodice. Both dolls now have a third version sewn-in label of white satin-type ribbon with "Terri Lee" in larger blue print. $450.00 – 600.00; more for dolls with braids or mint in box.

Two 16" hard plastic Terri Lee Girl Scouts with painted brown eyes with white highlights, painted lashes and brows, and closed pouty mouth. These second variations of Terri Lee Girl Scout uniform no longer have buttons but now use gripper type snap closures, and the sewn-on costume labels reading "Terri Lee" in blue print are now made of white satin-type ribbon. One variation has a much smaller white logo on the dark green felt hat while the other costume has the same larger Girl Scout emblem.

Second Terri Lee sewn-in label has blue printing on white, circa 1950 – 1955.

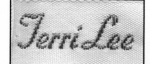

Third sewn-in label used by Terri Lee has blue embroidery on white and was used circa 1955 – 1959.

The Brownie uniforms also have variations. The oldest style has buttons and a pocket on the bodice and has a sewn-in white rayon label with blue print. The same fabric belt has a gripper snap closure and fits into belt loops sewn at the waist. The next variation has a different type of sewn-on label, now made of satin-type rayon and dates from 1950 – 1955.

Three 16" hard plastic Terri Lees with synthetic wigs, painted eyes with white highlights, painted lashes and brows, all with five-piece hard plastic bodies. All wear Brownie costumes of brown cotton with pocket on upper left bodice and brown felt beanie type hats. The first doll on the far left wears the first Brownie version with buttons and pocket on the bodice, has the rayon label with blue print, and is from the era 1947 – 1950. The middle and right versions have the second type sewn-in white satin-type label that reads "Terri Lee" in blue print. The date on these costumes is 1950 – 1955. $450.00 – 600.00.

Three 16" hard plastic Terri Lees with synthetic wigs, painted eyes with white highlights, painted lashes and brows, all with five-piece hard plastic bodies. All wear Brownie costumes of brown cotton with self-belt held in loops attached to the waist. All three dresses now open completely down the front, have lost the pocket on the left bodice and have smaller shirttail hems that are machine sewn. All three costumes have the white satin label with slighter larger blue print and date from 1955 – 1959. Some of the hats are no longer the beanie type but now are felt formed hats, price range from $450.00 – 600.00.

In 1955, the Terri Lee Company introduced Tiny Terri Lee. These dolls are 10" tall hard plastic walkers with sleep eyes with extra long eyelashes, painted brows, and closed pouty mouth. She is marked on the back with a ©. She was also costumed as a Girl Scout and Brownie. Her dress label is always the embroidered or woven tag in blue and white and marked Terri Lee. There are two different variations in both the Girl Scout and Brownie uniforms made for Tiny Terri Lee. Costumes come with visible front closure snap or with hidden snaps variations for both the Brownie and the Girl Scout.

Three 10" hard plastic Tiny Terri Lee dolls with extra long eyelashes, sleep eyes, closed pouty mouths, and synthetic wigs. They are marked on the back with a © symbol. The green cotton Girl Scout uniform on the left has hidden snaps but is also available with visible snaps. The brown cotton Brownie uniform in the center has visible snaps and the one on the far right has hidden snaps, circa 1955 – 1958. $200.00.

White paper tag found on 16" Terri Lee Girl Scouts and Brownies has a green Girl Scout trefoil emblem, "Uniforms approved by the Girl Scouts of the United States of America."

Original tan Terri Lee Box has brown printing.

Effanbee Doll Company, 1949 – 1957

This marked Effanbee hard plastic Honey with mohair wig, sleep eyes, and jointed five-piece body was made from 1949 – 1957. This example wears a homemade Brownies costume made from Brownie material. She is not official nor is the dressed Honey wearing a homemade Girl Scout costume.

14" hard plastic Effanbee Honey has a short mohair wig, brown plastic sleep eyes, closed mouth, and jointed marked hard plastic body and wears a homemade Brownie short-sleeved dress with matching belt of the same Brownie material and a felt hat. She has leatherette center-snap shoes and white socks. $150.00.

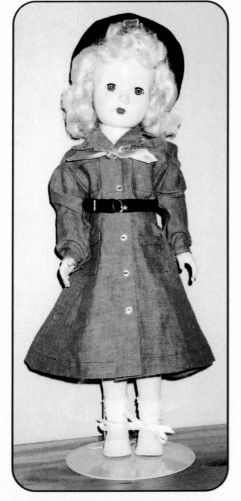

18" hard plastic Effanbee Honey has a blonde synthetic wig, blue plastic sleep eyes, closed mouth, and jointed marked hard plastic body and wears a well-made Girl Scout uniform with two pockets on the skirt, yellow ribbon tie, dark green vinyl belt, and a dark green felt hat with the Girl Scout logo. She has white leatherette tie shoes and white socks. $300.00.

Artisan Doll (Artisan Novelty Co.) circa 1950s

Artisan introduced the unmarked hard plastic Raving Beauty in 1950; one identifying tip is her unusually widespread legs with a walking mecha-nism. Her synthetic wig was "Ravon," and she has a wardrobe of "California Originals," costumes by Michele.

19" hard plastic Artisan Doll "Raving Beauty" with short blonde Ravon wig, brown sleep eyes with real lashes, open mouth and upper teeth, wears a homemade Brownie uniform with Brownie logo on bodice pocket and dark brown beanie style hat. The hat is made in four pieces and is lined. Shown with an American Girl accessory, a bicycle for Molly. Raving Beauty, circa 1950, $250.00.

Mimi Kay Specialties, Oak Park, Illinois, 1953

Mimi Kay kits offered in 1953 included an 8" felt doll and complete costume ready to cut, wool yarn for hair, embroidery floss, and step-by-step instructions, but no stuffing. There was a "Nancy Lee" costumed as a Brownie and "Susan Scout" as a Girl Scout. These dolls were not official.

8" felt Nancy Lee Brownie doll made from a Mimi Kay kit has yellow yarn hair, painted features, and a brown felt short-sleeved dress with pocket on upper bodice, matching belt, shoes, and beanie hat, $45.00. Photos courtesy Lynne Armstrong.

Instruction booklet included in Mimi Kay kit pictures Nancy Lee Brownie and Susan Scout and gives directions for making Susan Scout.

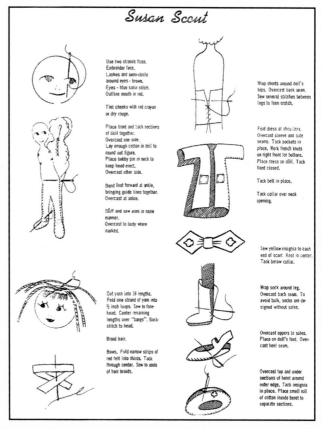

Uncut Mimi Kay Scout Kit that included pattern printed on felt, embroidery thread, and yarn for hair, $100.00. Courtesy Lynne Armstrong.

Two 8" unmarked hard plastic Cosmopolitan Ginger dolls, wigged and dressed by Terri Lee. The Girl Scout wears a green dress, opening down the front with snap button closures, felt hat, a matching green leatherette belt, and green socks with black plastic shoes. The Brownie wears a brown dress with button snap closures down the front, dark brown leatherette belt, socks, shoes, and a brown felt hat with Brownie logo. They are packed in boxes with alternating stripes of solid green or brown color and Girl Scout trefoil logos. Circa 1956 – 1958, prices for boxed dolls range $175.00 – 225.00.

Cosmopolitan Ginger, 1956 – 1958, dressed by Terri Lee

According to Peggy Casper in her book on Terri Lee dolls, Cosmopolitan Doll & Toy Corp., in Long Island, New York made an 8" Ginger little girl doll. Cosmopolitan also manufactured dolls for Fortune Toys, Inc, which made an 8" Ginger look-alike walker. They produced the 8" Girl Scout and Brownie dolls that were dressed in tagged Terri Lee uniform under a contract with the Girl Scout organization. The Terri Lee Ginger dolls have a similarly styled Raysheen wig as Terri Lee. These dolls were sold both by Terri Lee and the Girl Scouts. The dolls were not marked, but the costumes are labeled "Terri Lee" and first appeared in the Girl Scout catalogs in 1957.

8" unmarked hard plastic Cosmopolitan Ginger in Terri Lee tagged Brownie uniform with box, showing end of box markings, "TRADE MARK//GIRL GS SCOUTS//REG. U. S. PAT. OFF."

Five 8" hard plastic Cosmopolitan dressed Girl Scouts and Brownies, all tagged "Terri Lee." There are some differences in the belts and type of snaps used; the dolls did not have matching panties. Circa 1956 – 1958, prices for boxed dolls range $175.00 – 225.00.

Two Cosmopolitan 8" hard plastic dolls dressed by the Cosmopolitan Doll & Toy Corp. in the late 1950s. They used a different color on the Brownie uniforms and different style hats, and the dolls had matching panties. It is believed that the Girl Scouts did not officially license these dolls. The uniforms are tagged "Fashions for Ginger//Cosmopolitan Doll & Toy Corp//Jackson Heights, N.Y.//Trade Mark," $125.00 each.

Nancy Ann Storybook, circa 1957

In 1957, Nancy Ann Storybook dressed Muffie, an 8" hard plastic doll from their line in a Brownie uniform. The costume was "Camp Girl Number K46 Brown Camp Girl Outfit with matching cap. Outfit only $1.98." Muffie is a straight-legged walker doll with synthetic wig, sleep-eyes, closed mouth, and chubby type five-piece body. Some later variations had a vinyl head and /or bent knees. She is marked "STORYBOOK//DOLLS//CALIFORNIA//MUFFIE."

We assume that the 10" hard plastic Debbie doll by Nancy Ann Storybook also was introduced at that time with the Brownie outfit. Debbie is marked "NANCY ANN" and wears a tagged uniform. Debbie is very rare in this costume, and Muffie is hard to find. The smaller, painted bisque Nancy Ann Storybook dolls wearing homemade outfits are not official.

Two small 4½" and 5" plastic Nancy Ann Storybook dolls have painted eyes and mohair wigs. One has white molded painted shoes to ankle and the other painted-on black shoes with ankle strap. Both outfits are homemade Brownie costumes and not official. Dolls are circa 1950s, $75.00 and $100.00.

8" hard plastic Nancy Ann Storybook Muffie straight leg walker with blonde synthetic wig, marked "STORYBOOK//DOLLS//CALIFORNIA//MUFFIE," wears costume Camp Girl Number K46." All NASB uniforms shown have a white satin tag with blue print, "Styled by Nancy Ann//Nancy Ann Storybook Dolls, Inc.//San Francisco, California." Nancy Ann Storybook Dolls came with distinctive boxes such as this one with white background, pale blue dots, and Nancy Ann Storybook written in script letters, circa 1957+, not official. $200.00.

8" hard plastic Nancy Ann Storybook Muffie straight leg walker with dark blonde synthetic wig is marked "STORYBOOK//DOLLS//CALI-FORNIA//MUFFIE" and wears costume Camp Girl Number K46. The Brownie costume is a short-sleeved dress with three snap closures. Her felt beanie has elastic to hold it on under the chin. Muffie has painted eyelashes and brows, sleep eyes, and closed mouth, circa 1957+, not official, $200.00.

10" hard plastic Nancy Ann Storybook Debbie has a Saran wig, sleep eyes, and is a straight leg walker marked "NANCY ANN" on the back of the neck. Debbie's Brownie uniform consists of a one-piece brown short-sleeved dress with four gripper snap closures, brown vinyl shoes, white socks, and a felt Beanie with Brownie emblem, circa 1957, $200.00.

Three Vogue 8" hard plastic dolls including the far left, Wee Imp, wearing a Girl Scout uniform made in the mid-1950s. Wee Imp has a bright carrot-red synthetic wig and freckles on her nose, sleep eyes, and closed mouth. Her uniform is green cotton, yellow tie, darker green belt, and dark green felt hat. She wears brown plastic side-snap Ginny shoes with dark green socks. The center Ginny also wears a dark green cotton Girl Scout uniform with snap button closures, yellow ribbon tie, plastic hat with elastic chin strap, and the Ginny on the right has a dark green snap closure dress with dark green hat. These dolls are not official. Each, $225.00 – 250.00.

Vogue Ginny, 1956 – 1965

The Vogue Doll Company was started by Jennie H. Adler Graves who began by sewing doll clothes at home, dressing imported German dolls and selling them to a local department store. Graves started the Vogue Doll Shoppe in 1925 in her home in Somerville, Massachusetts. She employed home sewers at first and then in 1939 moved to Medford, Massachusetts and shortly had a building just for her doll business. Graves designed for her dolls for over 20 years and loved to include a hat with each costume.

After WWII, in 1945 Graves incorporated Vogue and moved to their first factory in Medford. Sales reportedly were $224,000.00 that year. In 1946, when sales declined, Graves decided to try a line of 8" hard plastic dolls that debuted in 1948. Commonwealth Plastics made the dolls as well as some accessories. The doll, named Ginny, originally sold for $1.98 in panties and slippers; 50 costumes were available. Sales jumped to over $2 million in 1953.

8" hard plastic Vogue Ginny with synthetic wig, blue sleep eyes, painted eyebrows, molded lashes, and closed mouth is wearing a light tan Girl Scout uniform and is tagged "Vogue Dolls//Medford Mass." This style dress has bright green snaps, green plastic belt, white socks, and green shoes. This costume is rarely found and is not official. $175.00 – 250.00. Photo courtesy Becky Byrns.

Four 8" Vogue hard plastic Ginny dolls in Brownie costume have synthetic wigs, sleep eyes, painted eyebrows, and closed mouths. All have tagged costumes, either "Vogue Dolls Inc.//Medford, Mass., U.S.A.//Reg. U.S. Pat. Off.", circa 1954 – 1956 or "Vogue Dolls, Inc." circa 1957 – mid 1960s. After 1957 the doll may have bent knees. The brown cotton uniform has snap button front closure, brown vinyl shoes, and matching brown felt hats with elastic to hold them under the chin. Not official. $175.00 – 250.00.

In 1957, Vogue employed 300 home sewers to provide costumes and was the largest doll manufacturer in the United States, with sales grossing over $5 million. Vogue acquired the Arranbee Doll Company in 1958, and Mrs. Graves retired in 1961. The company was sold out of the family's control in 1972 and went through a succession of owners. Vogue was purchased by Jim and Linda Smith in 1995 who have revitalized the company and brought back the wonderful costuming that originated with its founder.

Vogue advertised and 8" hard plastic Ginny with Brownie costume in their fashion booklets, and in the 1956 booklet, the Brownie costume is shown under "Gym Kids." It is not named and only has a stock number, #6132. It sold for $1.50 for the outfit alone or $3.50 for the dressed doll. Dolls had a sewn-on label that read "Vogue Dolls Inc.//Medford, Mass., U.S.A.//Reg. U.S. Pat. Off," circa 1954 – 1956. During the 1957 to the mid 1960s, Ginny dolls carried a label that read, "Vogue Dolls, Inc."

The Ginny doll was marked on the back "Ginny//Vogue Dolls, Inc.//Pat. Pend.//Made in U.S. A." during the production year of 1954. In 1955, Ginny is marked "VOGUE" on the head and "Ginny//Vogue Dolls, Inc.//Pat. No. 2687594//Made in the U.S.A." In 1957, bending knees were added, and the marks remained the same as the 1955 dolls.

Ginny Girl Scout dolls have also been found. It is not clear, whether or not Vogue produced the commercially-made costumes. Premier Doll Accessories Company did make Girl Scout costumes to fit 8" dolls.

Ravca, late 1940s – 1950s

7" cloth doll with painted features, painted shoes and socks, and mohair wig wears a Girl Scout uniform from the late 1940s to 1950s era. She carries a silver and blue tag that reads "Bernard Ravca//Paris New York." This doll is not officially licensed by the Girl Scouts. $100.00.

Silver paper tag reads: "Original RAVCA//Paris – New York" and is a hang-tag used by Ravca for his dolls.

5" Ravca-type Girl Scout has a crepe paper-wrapped wooden oval head. She has painted features and side-glancing eyes. Her Inter-mediate-style Scout uniform is crepe paper and also has a matching green hat on her brown crepe paper wig. She has a bright yellow crepe paper tie, green socks, and black shoes. This doll is not official. $50.00. Photo courtesy Mary Eskridge.

Imperial Crown Toy Company (IMPCO), circa 1950s

14" hard plastic unmarked IMPCO walker with extra piece in neck to allow the head to tilt at different angles. She has a dark gold synthetic wig with blue sleep eyes, an open/closed mouth, and painted brows. No tag in brown cotton short-sleeved Brownie dress that opens completely down the front. The bodice has a patch pocket, three snap buttons, matching panties. She wears a dark brown heavy felt hat; this costume is not official. $125.00.

Unknown Maker, 1950s

14" unmarked hard plastic doll with blonde mohair wig, sleep eyes, real lashes, and closed mouth wears a home-made brown cotton short-sleeved Brownie dress with dark brown felt cap, circa 1950s, $75.00.

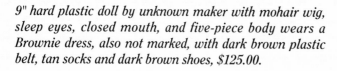

9" hard plastic doll by unknown maker with mohair wig, sleep eyes, closed mouth, and five-piece body wears a Brownie dress, also not marked, with dark brown plastic belt, tan socks and dark brown shoes, $125.00.

Transitions through the 1960s

Sayco Doll Corporation, late 1950s –1960s

Sayco Doll Corporation made dolls in the 1950s and 1960s, and one of their most notable was the Miss America Pageant Doll. The dolls can be unmarked, or marked with an "S" or "Sayco." It is believed they produced a Brownie in the late 1950s or early 1960s. She has a vinyl head with hard plastic body and rooted hair. The Brownie uniform is pictured in the Miss America Pageant Doll brochure as a "School Club outfit, with brown beanie, shoulder strap bag, brown dress, shoes and socks."

Sewn-in label from center back skirt seam of Sayco Brownie costume.

10¾" vinyl Sayco Miss America Pageant Doll in Brownie costume has sleep blue eyes, rooted hair, closed mouth, and a hard plastic body with jointed knees. Her brown dress is tagged in center back seam, "Miss America//Pageant Doll//Sayco Doll Corp//Brooklyn 11, N.Y." (above). Her belt is brown vinyl with gold buckle and matches her purse. The short-sleeved cotton dress fastens the front with two buttons. The Sayco Brownie is not official, $175.00. Photo courtesy Mary Eskridge.

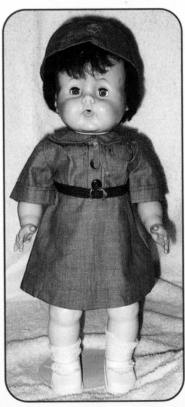

16½" Sayco marked doll wears a homemade cotton short-sleeved Brownie uniform of official Brownie material. The orange logo on her beanie style cap is embroidered. The doll is not official, $65.00. Photo courtesy Mary Eskridge.

Beehler Arts, Ltd. 1959 – 1964

Beehler Arts, Ltd. was reported to have had their dolls made by Ontario Plastics Company and are similar to dolls by Virga and Fortune. Circa 1959, Beehler Arts, Ltd. made an 8" hard plastic Brownie named Lucy. In 1960, they produced an 8" hard plastic Girl Scout. Their clothes are not tagged; inside the box lid reads, "Mfg. By Beehler Arts, Ltd. N.Y." The Beehler Arts Brownie can be identified by the white Brownie logo on her hat. Approximately 8,800 Brownies and 12,000 Junior Girl Scout dolls were produced.

8" hard plastic Beehler Arts, Ltd. Brownie wears tan cotton uniform with brown buttons, plastic belt. She has a dark brown felt beanie with white Brownie logo. The dolls have Buster Brown haircuts with bangs, sleep eyes, painted eyebrows, and matching brown plastic shoes and socks. These dolls came with brown boxes that have the Girl Scout logo and read: "Official//8"//Brownie Scout Doll." Inside the box lid reads "Mfg. By Beehler Arts, Ltd. N.Y." The dolls and the case are official. Price, mint in box, $125.00; the blue vinyl case made circa 1961 – 1964, $50.00 – 100.00.

8" hard plastic Virga with bent knees and marked box, "Beautiful//Virga//Dolls//Play-mates" and also "P-833 Camp Girl//Bending Knee" and "Manufactured by Beehler Arts, LTD//47 West St., New York City." She has sleep eyes, closed mouth, painted brows, and synthetic wig. She wears a green Girl Scout long-sleeved dress with white gripper snap button at waist, green socks, black vinyl shoes, and dark green felt hat, circa 1956 – 1957, not official, $225.00.

Uneeda Doll Co., circa 1961 – 1963

Uneeda Doll Co., New York City, started circa 1917 and made composition dolls for resale for catalog companies and retail stores. The company survived the changeover from composition to plastic and vinyl and made numerous dolls over the years including the multi-jointed fashion type "Dollikin."

During the period 1961 – 1963, Uneeda produced 8" hard plastic Brownie and Girl Scout dolls. They are usually marked with a small "U" on the back of the neck. The dolls appear identical to the 8" hard plastic Beehler Arts dolls. Both dolls have sleep eyes, closed mouths, and Buster Brown haircuts. Some of the Uneeda doll costumes have fake buttons on their uniforms while others have no buttons. One difference is that the Brownie doll's hat has the Brownie logo screened on in orange while Beehler's has a white logo. The Brownie's name is "Janie," and 55,400 Brownie dolls were made along with 17,834 Junior Girl Scout dolls. They also come in a brown lidded box that reads, "Official//8"//Brownie Scout Doll."

8" hard plastic Uneeda Brownie Janie with synthetic Buster Brown wig, sleep eyes, closed mouth, and jointed five-piece body can be distinguished from the Beehler Arts Brownie by the orange Brownie logo on her hat. Her brown cotton uniform has a shirt-like collar, short sleeves, narrow hem, buttons on bodice, brown plastic belt and shoes, and brown socks, circa 1961 – 1963. Official, mint in box, $125.00.

Two 8" Uneeda Junior Girl Scouts with red and blonde Buster Brown wigs, marked "U" on the back of their neck, they have painted eyebrows, molded eyelashes, and blue sleep eyes. They have dark green snaps down the front of the green cotton long-sleeved dresses with plastic belts, brown plastic shoes, and green socks. Their beanie cap has the white trefoil logo with the "GS" initials. Official, mint in box, $35.00 – 100.00.

Effanbee, 1959 – 1979

Effanbee had a 20-year production contract for official licensed Girl Scout dolls. In 1959 they produced a vinyl 15" vinyl Patsy Ann with freckled face that would soon sport Girl Scout and Brownie uniforms. Circa 1961 – 1963, they dressed the 15" vinyl Suzette as a Girl Scout and Brownie. It is sometimes difficult to find them complete. The clothing is made from official material. Suzette is perhaps harder to find than Patsy Ann. These dolls are advertised in Effanbee catalogs in 1959, in the Sears Christmas catalog in 1962, and also can be found on page 14 of the 1966/67 Girl Scout catalog. Those with the golden paper heart tag also sport the Girl Scout trefoil emblem and say they are a Girl Scout or a Brownie. They are official.

Two 15" vinyl Effanbee marked "Patsy Ann" dolls with blue sleep eyes, synthetic rooted hair, painted eyebrows, freckles across nose and cheeks, closed mouths, and jointed bodies. The Girl Scout wears a short-sleeved green cotton uniform that buttons down the front, matching panties, green vinyl belt, brown shoes, and green socks. Her dark green hat has a white trefoil emblem with the initials, G.S. She wears a yellow scarf at the neck. Both dolls are marked on the head "EFFANBEE//PATSY ANN//©1959" and marked on the back "EFFANBEE." The 15" vinyl Patsy Ann Brownie wears a brown cotton dress with three buttons down the front, matching panties, a brown vinyl belt, brown felt beanie, brown socks, and black shoes. Her gold paper heart-shaped tag claims. "I am//The Official//Brownie//An//Effanbee//Durable//Doll." $200.00 – 350.00.

Two 15" all-vinyl Effanbee Suzettes with rooted synthetic hair, sleep eyes, and jointed bodies. The Girl Scout wears a green cotton short-sleeved dress with buttons down the front, matching panties, green vinyl belt, green socks, black shoes, and a dark green felt hat. The Suzette Brownie wears a brown cotton short-sleeved dress with orange ribbon tie, brown vinyl belt, buttons to the waist, dark brown socks, shoes, and beanie. She carries a gold paper heart-shaped tag reads "I am//The Official//Brownie//An//Effanbee//Durable//Doll." $200.00 – 400.00.

In 1964 the Girl Scout catalogs show another Effanbee doll, the 8" vinyl Fluffy. Fluffy is possibly the easiest doll to locate, and her size varies from 8" to 9". She was carried in the Girl Scout catalogs until 1974. In 1968, Effanbee produced a black version of Fluffy Girl Scout and Brownie. Quoting from *The Girl Scout Collectors Guide*, there were 212,900 white Fluffy Brownies dolls, 91,800 white Girl Scouts, 12,600 black Brownies, and 9,600 black Girl Scouts produced during this period.

8" vinyl Effanbee "Fluffy" with synthetic rooted hair, sleep eyes with real lashes and painted lashes below, painted eyebrows, closed mouth, and jointed vinyl body. The Girl Scout costume is a green cotton short-sleeved dress with button front closure. She has a yellow satin ribbon tie, green socks, dark brown plastic shoes, green socks, green felt hat with white Girl Scout logo, and green vinyl belt. The Fluffy Brownie has a brown cotton short-sleeved dress, with brown vinyl belt, brown socks and shoes, an orange ribbon tie, and dark brown beanie with orange Brownie logo, $25.00 – 75.00.

Close-up shows face of 8" vinyl Effanbee "Fluffy" with synthetic rooted hair, sleep eyes with real lashes and painted lashes below, painted eyebrows, closed mouth, and jointed vinyl body.

61

Effanbee presented Fluffy in three different boxes, a plastic top, a shrink-wrap, and a pink checked box with see-through window. The pink box is harder to find. Fluffy also was produced in a camp uniform and a swimsuit. These all show the imprinted Girl Scout logo.

The Girl Scout catalogs in both 1963 and 1965 show an official 11" all vinyl Effanbee Fluffy. She came with a gold paper Effanbee heart tag and was packed in a green box that reads, "Official//Cadette//Girl Scout Doll."

Effanbee also produced the 11" Fluffy as the 1965 Roundup doll. This official doll was produced in a very limited amount, making the Roundup Fluffy very hard to find. She is dressed in the official Roundup uniform and is hard to find in the box.

Effanbee used three different boxes for the 8" vinyl Fluffy Girl Scouts and Brownies. They were plastic shrink-wrapped boxes, brown and green boxes with heavier plastic see-through lids, and pink checked cardboard boxes with plastic see-through windows. The pink box is more rare; mint in box doll, $125.00; with pink box, $200.00.

Four 8" vinyl Effanbee Fluffy in camp uniforms and swimsuits. On the left, a blonde Fluffy wears a turquoise and white swimsuit with stamped Girl Scout logo. In the left center, Fluffy wears a camp uniform with white blouse with Girl Scout logo and dark green shorts, green socks, and brown vinyl shoes. In right center, Fluffy wears an orange and white swimsuit with the Brownie logo stamped on the pants of the suit. On the far right, Fluffy wears a white shirt with Brownie logo and brown shorts with brown socks and shoes. Swimsuit, $50.00; shirt and short set, $65.00.

11" vinyl Effanbee Fluffy, all original in green and white Cadette uniform, with rooted blonde hair, sleep eyes, and closed mouth. She wears a white blouse with green ribbon tie and a green skirt with white Girl Scout logo. Her hat is of matching green fabric and has red, green, and white ribbon trim. She carries a gold paper heart Effanbee label, and her dark green box is marked "Cadette" inside a Girl Scout logo in a circle and "Official//Cadette//Girl Scout Doll." Mint in box, $600.00.

11" vinyl Effanbee Fluffy made especially for the 1962 Roundup wears a white blouse and dark green shorts. She has a brown vinyl belt and shoes and green socks. She wears a lanyard and a straw hat with round Roundup logo. The hat ties with yellow satin ribbon. $400.00. Courtesy Lynne Armstrong.

11" vinyl Effanbee Fluffy made especially for the 1965 Roundup wears a white blouse and dark green shorts. She has a brown vinyl belt and shoes and green socks. She wears a lanyard and a straw hat with round Roundup logo. The hat ties on with yellow satin ribbon. Mint in box, $650.00.

Changes in the 1970s

Effanbee

A new Junior Girl Scout and Brownie were first shown in the 1974 Girl Scout catalog. An 8" Fluffy was on sale there for $2.50. The Fluffy Camp Uniform and bathing suit sold in the same catalog for 55 cents. The new 11" vinyl dolls were by Effanbee, and they sold for $8.50 each. The doll used was one from Effanbee's line called Pun'kin. Pun'kin was produced from 1966 – 1983. She is described as "an all vinyl toddler, fully jointed with moving eyes and rooted hair that can be washed and combed." The head is marked "EFFANBEE//19©66".

The uniforms were changed to match the new style uniforms for the Junior Girl Scout, and Brownie. For the Junior Girl Scout this is a green cotton jumper, white logo patterned short-sleeved white blouse with red tie, black vinyl shoes, green socks, and dark green hat with white Girl Scout emblem. The emblem changed on both the Girl Scout and the Brownie in 1979. The Brownie doll is similar in brown jumper with brown and white patterned short-sleeved blouse, and brown beanie hat with orange emblem. Both dolls also carry the gold paper Effanbee tag. They came in brown or green boxes that read: "Girl (emblem G. S.) Scout//Official Brownie (or Junior) Girl Scout Doll." *The Girl Scout Collector's Guide* quotes surprising numbers in that more Junior Scout dolls (15, 280) as compared to 3,728 Brownie dolls were sold. Usually the Brownie dolls sold in higher numbers.

Two 11" all-vinyl Effanbee Junior Girl Scout and Brownie dolls show the change of uniforms in 1974. The Junior Girl Scout has a green cotton jumper worn over a short-sleeved green and white pattern blouse with rounded Peter Pan collar and red ribbon tie. Pun'kin has rooted dark hair, sleep eyes, painted eyebrows, a delicate pink colored mouth, and vinyl body. She wears black shoes and dark green socks and has a dark green hat with white Girl Scout emblem logo. The Pun'kin Brownie has the same style uniform with a brown jumper, brown and white pattern blouse, orange tie, and dark brown beanie with orange logo. She has dark brown shoes and brown socks. Both dolls are marked on the head, "EFFANBEE." Mint in box, $50.00 – 100.00.

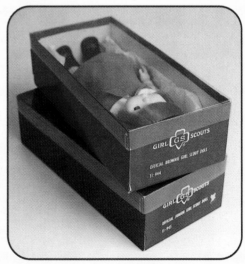

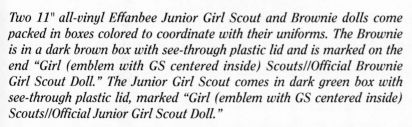

Two 11" all-vinyl Effanbee Junior Girl Scout and Brownie dolls come packed in boxes colored to coordinate with their uniforms. The Brownie is in a dark brown box with see-through plastic lid and is marked on the end "Girl (emblem with GS centered inside) Scouts//Official Brownie Girl Scout Doll." The Junior Girl Scout comes in dark green box with see-through plastic lid, marked "Girl (emblem with GS centered inside) Scouts//Official Junior Girl Scout Doll."

Hallmark Cards, Kansas City, Missouri

At age 16, Joyce C. Hall and his two older brothers started a postcard company. At age 18, despite his parents' objections, he dropped out of school, took a couple of boxes of postcards, and hit the road trying to sell them. He had little money, but a big dream and after 90 years, Hallmark Cards, based in Kansas City, Missouri, is still going strong.

Hallmark Cards produced a doll series in the 1970s. They dolls are silk-screened on cloth, approximately 6" tall. Linda Edwards in her book *Cloth Dolls, Ancient to Modern*, relates that the first series in 1976 were Bicentennial Commemoratives dolls and included George and Martha Washington, Benjamin Franklin, and Betsy Ross. In 1979 Hallmark made a series of Famous Americans that included George Washington Carver, Chief Joseph, Susan B. Anthony, Amelia Earhart, Babe Ruth, and Annie Oakley. A second series of Famous Americans portrayed Mark Twain, P.T. Barnum, Juliette Gordon Low, Davy Crockett, Clara Barton, and Molly Pitcher. The second series was available through a mail-order special offer, and only a few were shipped directly to Hallmark stores. They came packaged in a small box that had graphics relating to the doll. Biographical information was printed on the inside of the boxes. This was the first commercially-made Juliette Low doll, although it was not official.

6" silk-screened cloth Hallmark Juliette Low doll, part of a series of Famous Americans issued in 1979. Juliette wears a tan two-piece dress with belt, brown hat, and black boots. Her features and details of her clothing are printed, and the clothing is not removable. She is tagged with a white label that reads "August, 1979/Maine N. 96/Mass Lic. No. 196/Ohio 6347 Mo./Reg. No. Pa. 252/Contents/Al New Material/Cotton And/SyntheticFibers." The other side of the label reads "© Hallmark Cds. Inc./K. C. Mo. 64141/Made in Taiwan/400DT114-3/Juliette Low/Doll Toy/Non-Washable." $50.00 – 65.00.

An interesting accessory from the 1970s is a plastic carry box for dolls that folds into a tent. The box is 12½" long x 9¼" wide and 3" deep. It is marked on the back "A Hallmark Toy//by Jilmar Co., Brooklyn, NY//Made in Taiwan." Closed, the cover shows camping scenes. This is not an official Girl Scout accessory, $25.00.

1980s Era

Dakin, 1983, San Francisco

R. Dakin & Co., a plush and cloth doll and toy maker located in San Francisco, also bought Vogue dolls and made Ginny dolls circa 1985 – 1996. One of their cloth dolls was a 14" Girl Scout produced in both white and black versions. It is unknown if this doll was officially sanctioned by the Girl Scouts USA.

14" cloth Dakin Girl Scouts with yarn hair, painted features, and some of the clothing sewn on to make the body. A sewn-on label reads "©R. Dakin & Co. – 1983//San Francisco, Ca.//PA Reg No. 118//All new Materials//Contents Polyester//A Product of Korea." $25.00 – 50.00. Courtesy Donie Oldhan.

Two 14" cloth Dakin Girl Scouts with yarn hair, painted features, and some of the clothing sewn on to make the body. A sewn-on label reads, "©R. Dakin & Co. – 1983//San Francisco, Ca.//PA Reg No. 118//All new Materials//Contents Polyester//A Product of Korea." Her hangtag reads "Dream Dolls by Dakin for ages 3 and up 'She's a Winner//She's a Girl Scout' #80-0003//Girl Scout." Came as either black or white cloth Scout. $25.00 – 50.00. Courtesy Donie Oldhan.

JESCO, 1985

The Cameo Doll Company was started in 1922 by Joseph L. Kallus who had founded the Rex Doll Co. in 1916. World War I ended his business since he was in the military. Earlier he had been a protégé of Rose O'Neill and had worked with O'Neill and Borgfelt to develop her Kewpies. With Cameo, he continued his association with Borgfelt and O'Neill and made composition Kewpies and composition Bye-Lo dolls. Cameo, along with Effanbee and Ideal, was one of the three major doll companies that made their own composition dolls in their own factories. Kallus sold Cameo in 1970 to Strombecker, and in 1982 Jesco acquired the rights to produce Kewpies.

In 1985 Jesco produced 10" dolls dressed in outfits to represent Junior Girl Scouts and Brownies; they are not official. The clothes are marked "Katie Klothes//Jesco." The clothes were sold separately from the doll and were available for about five years.

Two 10" vinyl Jesco dolls with long synthetic hair, sleep eyes, closed smiling mouths, pale lip color, painted brows, and real lashes. The Girl Scout uniform had a green and pink shirt with green skirt, green hat, white vinyl shoes that tie, and white stockings. She has a green sash with badges. The Brownie wears a dark brown jumper with tan checked blouse, red ribbon tie, brown hat, and tan sash with badges. She also has white vinyl shoes and socks. $50.00 – 75.00.

Girl Scouts USA, 1985

The 1984/1985 Girl Scout catalog lists an 11½" cloth Brownie doll. She is one-piece cloth with her clothing printed on the body. In the 1984/1985 catalog, this Brownie is priced at $11.00. In the 1985/1986 catalog, she is on sale with the price of $8.00. Her printed-on uniform consists of a brown jumper, white striped blouse with orange tie, brown sash, brown socks, and black shoes. She wears her brown beanie hat with orange Girl Scout logo and has two ponytails with orange bows. Her features and hair are printed with brown eyes, eyelashes, eyebrows, and an open mouth with teeth. She is tagged "Product of USA." She came in a clear plastic bag that had green and blue stripes on the top, reading "Brownie Girl Scout Doll" and is official.

11½" preprinted and stuffed cloth Girl Scout Brownie, one-piece body with brown printed hair and features. She has brown side-glancing eyes with white highlights, open mouth with teeth, and two brown ponytails with orange bows. Her uniform is a brown jumper with sash, brown striped blouse, orange tie, brown hat with orange Girl Scout logo, and brown socks with black shoes. She was packaged in a clear plastic bag with label. She is tagged "Product of USA." $20.00 – 45.00.

In 1987, Dakin produced an official Girl Scout doll. She was a 12" all-cloth dressed in a replica of the uniform used in the early years of 1912 – 1914. The Burry Lu Cookie Company issued it. The doll has a hangtag that portrays a blue uniformed scout holding a banner that reads "1912 – 1987." The back of the tag reads "80-0020//Commemorative//Doll//© 1986 R. Dakin, San Francisco, Ca. Product of Korea." This doll was made to celebrate the 75th anniversary of Girl Scouts. The doll is unusual in that some of the faces are blue and some are white. The doll has painted eyes, lashes, pale pink lip color, brown yarn hair, stitched fingers, blue hat and dress, light blue tie, and brown sewn-on shoes. This is an official doll.

12" all-cloth Dakin "Burry Lu" commemorative Girl Scout dressed in blue uniform of the 1912 – 1914 era and celebrating the 75th anniversary of the founding of the Girl Scout organization. Some have blue faces; some have white with painted features, pale pink lip color, and are dressed in dark blue dress and hat with light blue tie. She has a hangtag with a blue Scout in graphics holding a gold banner that reads, "1912 – 1987". The back of the tag reads "80-0020//Commemorative//Doll//©1986 R. Dakin, San Francisco, Ca. Product of Korea." $75.00.

Home Shopping Club, 1989

In 1989, the Home Shopping Club (now known as HSN) introduced a doll by Marion Yu Design Company. She was called "Veronica" and sold as a Girl Scout. She is dressed in a khaki uniform with two button-down pockets on the bodice, side pockets in the skirt, brown belt, and red tie. She has a military type hat, tan knee stockings, and black "Mary Jane" style shoes. Her head, arms, and legs are porcelain, and she is 19" tall. She has blue eyes, painted brows, closed mouth, and wears a golden synthetic wig in ponytails tied with red ribbons. This is not an official doll.

19½" porcelain Marion Yu Design Company's Veronica with blue eyes, painted brows, and closed mouth. She has a gold synthetic wig in ponytails with red ribbons. She is marked "600/1000/MYD-inc./MarionYuDesign©." She has porcelain arms and legs, and the torso is cloth. Her uniform is a short-sleeved khaki tan dress with two button-down pockets on the bodice, a brown belt held in fitted loops, and side pockets in the skirt. She wears tan knees socks and black "Mary Jane" style shoes. $45.00 – 85.00.

Cabbage Patch, Coleco Industries, West Hartford, CT, 1983+

The Cabbage Patch phenomenon started in 1978 when Xavier Roberts began Babyland General Hospital and offered soft sculptured dolls. When demands for the "Little People" increased, Roberts licensed Coleco Industries to mass-produce Cabbage Patch Kids. The doll was designed in vinyl by Judith Albert and introduced in 1983. They came in green and yellow boxes with cellophane windows and included an adoption paper and birth certificate with individualized names.

While there was no official connection to the Girl Scout organization, some entrepreneurial dealers, such as Hobby City in southern California, sold Brownie and Girl Scout costumes for the Cabbage Patch Kids. Originally, the uniforms sold for about $25.00 each for the uniform only, the doll was extra.

16" vinyl Coleco Cabbage Patch Kids with decal eyes, yarn hair, closed smiling mouths, and cloth bodies, dressed in various versions of Brownie and Girl Scout costumes from jumpers with blouses to skirts and vests with matching blouses. These uniforms were not licensed; $25.00 each.

1990s through the Present

Ladie and Friends, Inc.

In 1990, Ladie and Friends, Inc. offered this Lizzie High all-wooden doll. Her tag reads, "Marlene Valentine couldn't find a thing on chipped shells in her Forest Friends First Aid Manual...No matter, 'Rule #1: A Forest Friend is always resourceful.' Our whimsical wooden folk dolls are an updated version of handcrafted ones from the past...and to personalize each doll, we have lovingly borrowed the wonderful names from our own family. We fondly introduce you to the family and friends of Lizzie High®dolls."

The back of tag reads "This Lizzie High ® doll was handcrafted for you by Debe and Doraty Zalnosli. The blank round face with two dots for eyes on the Lizzie High ® dolls/ is a trademark of Ladie & Friends, Inc./©Ladie & Friends, Inc. 1990." The doll has painted features and red braids, red check scarf, white blouse, and brown skirt. She sits on a wooden bench and is giving first aid to a turtle. This is not an official licensed doll of Girl Scouts USA.

10" Ladie and Friends all-wooden doll seated on bench, holds injured turtle and first aid kit on her lap. She has painted features, red pigtails, brown hat, brown skirt, and red scarf and is tagged "Marlene Valentine couldn't find a thing on chipped shells in the Forest Friends First Aid Manual …..No Matter, Rule Number 1. A Forest Friend is always resourceful," $100.00.

Dakin, 1992

Dakin produced a limited edition of 2,016 vinyl 80th Anniversary Daisy Ginnys for Girl Scouts USA. Each one came with a certificate and is numbered. They came in both black and white versions with blonde braids or black hair. They have a gold ribbon across their blue cotton long-sleeved uniforms with dark blue cuffs. There are two dark blue pockets on the bodice and two on the skirts. She has a dark blue hat and black button-up boots. Included with the doll are a small box of cookies and a small 1912 handbook.

8" black vinyl Dakin Ginny "Anniversary Daisy" with five-piece jointed body, sleep eyes with molded lashes, and rooted black hair, marked on the back "VOGUE © DOLLS//© 1984 R. DAKIN INC. //Made in China." She wears a light blue dress with dark blue pockets and hat and black high-button boots. Accessories include small box of cookies and 1912 Girl Scout handbook. Mint in box, $125.00.

8" vinyl Dakin Ginny "Anniversary Daisy" with five-piece jointed body, sleep eyes with molded lashes, rooted blonde pigtails and marked on the back "VOGUE ©DOLLS//©1984 R. DAKIN INC. //Made in China." She wears a light blue dress with dark blue pockets and hat and black high button boots. Accessories include a small box of cookies and 1912 Girl Scout handbook. Mint in box, $125.00.

Certificate of Authenticity for the 80th Anniversary Commemorative Ginny Daisy Doll was signed by the executive director of the Girl Scout Council and issued with each doll.

Premium Pixie Doll

Cookie sales have been a fund-raising activity for years, and sometimes there were premiums that went along with the cookie campaigns. In 1995, the premium was an 11½" vinyl Pixie doll dressed in blue and green with a peaked green cap. This doll was unmarked, and it may be assumed this was an official doll since there was a Certificate of Authenticity with the doll that reads, "This Limited Edition Brownie Doll was created by Ross K. Bennett of Red Pepper Productions, Inc. for a Girl Scout Cookie Premium. The production of this doll was limited to 13,000 pieces with the last piece produced in December, 1995." The doll was presented in a clear plastic bag.

Certificate of Authenticity came with each pixie-type Brownie and stated, "This Limited Edition Brownie Doll was created by Ross K. Bennett of Red Pepper Productions, Inc. for a Girl Scout Cookie Premium. The production of this doll was limited to 13,000 pieces with the last piece produced in December, 1995."

11½" Red Pepper Productions vinyl Brownie with synthetic wig uses an adult fashion-type body. She wears a peaked green hat, short-sleeved blue shirt with green bodice and blue collar, blue overskirt, and long green tights with blue cloth shoes. This was a premium doll for Girl Scout cookie sales by Red Pepper Productions with a limited edition of 13,000, made only in 1995, $15.00 – 30.00.

Madame Alexander Doll Company

Madame Alexander Doll Company was begun by Beatrice and Rose Alexander around 1912 when they were already well known for their expertise in costuming dolls. They began using the Madame Alexander trademark in 1928. Beatrice Alexander Behrmann became a legend in the doll world with a long reign as head of the company that produced cloth, composition, and wood dolls and made the transition into hard plastic and vinyl after WWII. They were fortunate to obtain the license to produce Scarlett O'Hara and the Dionne Quintuplets during the 1930s which further boosted their success. The company reorganized after bankruptcy and is again one of the leading doll companies producing a wide range of dolls.

In 1992, Madame Alexander made an 8" hard plastic doll called Scouting. Production was halted on the doll that same year when a license infringement was discovered, but a number of them had already been sold. They are not official.

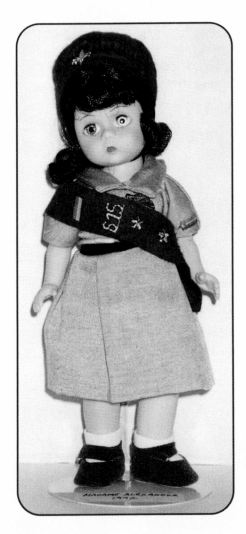

8" hard plastic Madame Alexander "Scouting" with black wig, closed mouth, sleep eyes, painted brows, and five-piece body. She wears a green short-sleeved dress with a darker green sash and dark green hat. She wears black shoes with white socks. This doll is not official. Mint in box, $125.00; more for blonde version.

Girl Scouts, USA, 1994 – Present

The 1994 Girl Scout catalog sold a Brownie costume to fit the 18" dolls such as the American Girls by the Pleasant Company. The costume for the Brownie was a blue shirt and brown shorts and you could make a hat to match. In 1996, the catalog offered an additional brown sweater. The 1995 – 1996 catalog offered a Girl Scout uniform with green shorts, white top, and socks. You could make a sash to match the uniform, and there was also a green sweater available. These Brownie and Girl Scout outfits are sold through the Girl Scout catalogs.

18" vinyl Pleasant Company American Girl "Kirsten" with vinyl arms and legs and cloth torso, also has sleep eyes, blonde synthetic wig in braids, and closed mouth. She wears an official Girl Scout uniform with a short-sleeved white blouse patterned by the initials "GS" in green and green cotton shorts. She wears the sash with her badges that is made at home to finish the costume. Doll, $84.00; costume $22.00, retail.

18" black vinyl Pleasant Company American Girl "Addy" with rooted long black wig, dark brown sleep eyes, and open/closed mouth with teeth is wearing the 1994 Brownie outfit with brown shorts with floral jumper-top and blue shirt. This official costume includes a pattern for a hat. Doll $84.00; outfit $22.00, retail.

Green Girl Scout or brown Brownie sweaters were also available. Sweaters, $15.00 each.

18" vinyl Pleasant Company American Girl "Kirsten" with rooted long blonde wig, blue sleep eyes, and open/closed mouth with teeth is wearing an artist version of the Girl Scout Daisy outfit with white shirt with embroidered daisies, "Daisy Girl Scout" in blue letters, and matching dark blue shorts. She also has a matching dark blue apron with "Daisy Girl Scout" in white lettering. Doll, $84.00; wheelchair, $30.00; outfit $45.00.

18" vinyl Pleasant Company American Girl "Felicity" with rooted red synthetic wig, green sleep eyes, open/closed mouth with teeth, vinyl arms and legs, and cloth torso wears an official pair of Girl Scout shorts and vest with white long-sleeved T-shirt, made in 1996. This costume is no longer available. Doll, $84.00; 1996 costume on eBay, $55.00 – 65.00.

18" vinyl Pleasant Company American Girl "Kirsten" with rooted long blonde wig, blue sleep eyes, and open/closed mouth with teeth is wearing an official Cadette/Senior Girl Scout uniform with blue and yellow stripes on white cotton and polyester blend blouse and bright royal blue shorts with blue sash. Doll, $84.00; outfit #11801 in 1999 – 2000 catalog, retail $22.50. It comes with a pattern for making a sash for your doll.

18" vinyl Pleasant Company American Girl "Samantha" with dark brown synthetic rooted hair, open/closed mouth with teeth, brown sleep eyes, vinyl arms and legs, and cloth torso wears a green sweatshirt with matching green multicolor patterned leggings. An official outfit, it is available in the 1997/1998 catalogs. The Pleasant Company doll is $84.00, and the costume is $24.00.

18" vinyl Pleasant Company American Girl "Josephina" with black synthetic hair, open/closed mouth with teeth, black sleep eyes, vinyl arms and legs, and cloth torso wears a blue Brownie costume of sweatshirt and leggings available in 1997/1998 catalog. An official outfit, the Pleasant Company doll is $84.00, and the costume is $24.00.

18" vinyl Pleasant Company American Girl "Molly" with dark brown synthetic rooted hair, open/closed mouth with teeth, blue sleep eyes, vinyl arms and legs, and cloth torso is advertised as a girl from the 1940s. She wears a copy of the author's camp outfit from the 1950s, dark green baggy shorts, and white shirt. This is not an official outfit. The Pleasant Company doll is $84.00, and the costume is $25.00.

Avon Products 1995

David McConnell, 28, of New York City discovered that the rose oil perfumes he was giving away were the reason people were buying his books and founded the California Perfume Company in New York. His first laboratory was 3,000 square feet on three floors. By 1971, Avon's research facility covers 323,000 square feet. In 1914 the California Perfume Company opened its first foreign office in Quebec, Canada. After World War I, sales reached $2 million, and he had 25,000 representatives selling products in the U.S.

Mrs. Persis Foster Eames Albee of Winchester New Hampshire, pioneered the company's now-famous direct-selling method. Married to a U.S. senator, she had worked with McConnell in his door-to-door book sales company part-time while raising her family. At that company, they gave out free small perfumes as a gift with their books. When McConnell realized that the perfume was more popular than the books, he founded the California Perfume Company and called on his former colleague to be his first representative. She agreed and took up what was, in effect, a second career, selling and recruiting others to sell McConnell's products. She traveled by horse and carriage all over the Northeast for many years. Today, with sales representatives numbering three and a half million, Avon Products are sold in 143 countries around the world. Women have been selling Avon since 1886, 34 years before American women won the right to vote!

In 1937, after McConnell's death, his son David Jr. became president. Products carried the Good Housekeeping Seal of Approval and in 1939, the company name was changed to Avon Products, Inc., named after McConnell's favorite playwright's homeplace, Stratford on Avon. In 1944, Avon was grossing almost $16 million a year. The company went public

in 1946. In 1954, Avon had 3,700 employees and advertised on television with "Avon Calling" and began developing business overseas, In 1963, domestic sales were $250 million and passed $750 million in 1970, reaching $3 billion in 1979. Sales were flat in the 1980s, but topped $5 billion in 1997.

In 1995, Avon offered "The Tender Memories" series with a 14" vinyl Girl Scout doll designed by Kathy Jeffers. She had red rooted hair, closed mouth, plastic eyes, and painted brows with green Girl Scout shorts, vest, and hat with print shirt and blue tie. She also wore dark green socks and brown shoes and carried a yellow cookie box. A black Girl Scout was also available. This was an official doll and came with paperwork, a stand, and an original box.

14" Avon vinyl Girl Scout cookie seller, with red rooted hair, plastic eyes, painted brows, and closed mouth. She wears a green and blue print blouse with dark blue tie, green vest, and green shorts with matching green hat with white Girl Scout logo. She has green socks and brown plastic shoes. $30.00; black version $35.00.

Barbie Costumes, 1995 – 2001

The Girl Scout catalogs 1995 through 2001 offered official uniforms for Barbie and her friends. Barbie became a Girl Scout Leader, and Skipper and her friends became Brownies and Juniors. The official costumes came in kit form and had to be sewn together. The original advertisement in the 1997/1998 catalogs listed them: "Brownie, Junior & Adult Girl Scout Uniform Sewing Craft Kits. Make your own doll uniforms. Each kit includes everything you need for two uniforms. Brownie/Junior kits designed to fit all 10" dolls (like Skipper®). Adult kit fits all 11½" dolls (like Barbie®). Dolls/thread not included. Complete with instructions. Adult Girl Scout Doll Craft Kit 18442 $9.25B. Brownie Girl Scout Doll Craft Kit. 18441 $9.25 C. Junior Girl Scout Doll Craft Kit 18440 $9.25."

Costume sets to fit the 11½" vinyl Mattel Barbie and 10" Skipper were offered in the Girl Scout catalog 1995 – 2001 and sold for $9.25.

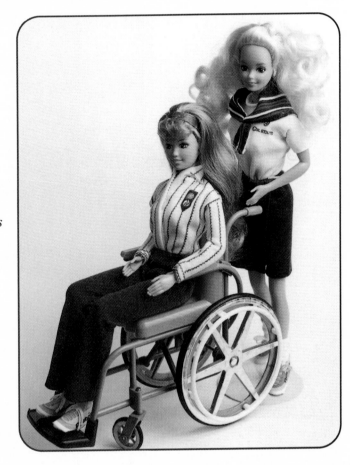

Barbie in Girl Scout and Leader costumes available in kits from Girl Scouts U.S.A.

11½" Mattel vinyl refurbished Barbie, with one-of-a-kind outfit to represent a Girl Scout wearing green and white logo blouse, long green slacks, sash, green earrings, and new box. This is not an official Girl Scout doll. $20.00.

Mary Hoyer Play doll, mid 1990s

14" vinyl Mary Hoyer play doll with synthetic wig, set plastic eyes, and closed mouth is a modern copy of the original. Mary had great accessories such as the tent and sleeping bag. Dressed as a Senior Scout, she is not officially authorized. Doll only, $70.00; costume, $20.00 – 35.00.

San Francisco Bay Area Council

A group of all-cloth Girl Scout dolls: 10¾" Julie the Daisy, 11" Savannah the Brownie, 11" Georgia the Junior Girl Scout, 12" Daisy the Cadette, 13¼" Millie the Senior Girl Scout, and a 14½" Leader. A Juliette in khaki is planned as the next doll. These dolls were made by the Girl Scouts of San Francisco Bay Area Council and given as "thank you" gifts for donations to Friends of Girl Scouting, beginning in 1996/1997. The dolls are faceless so that girls could fill in the faces and personalize them. All have the Friends of Girl Scouting pin for that year on their hats and are all marked "S.F. Bay," "San Francisco Bay Girl Scout Council" or "Girl Scouts of San Francisco Bay." These are official dolls given for a donation of $50.00 or more. Photo courtesy Lynne Armstrong.

Troll-type, late 1990s

3" vinyl one-piece troll by unknown maker has blue hair and blue plastic eyes and wears tan cotton uniform with a red tie. She wears a matching tan hat with printed letters "Troll Scouts." This is not an authorized Girl Scout doll. $5.00.

Girl Scout USA Catalog, 1997 – 1999

Cloth Daisy Brownie doll with printed features was available in the 1998/1999 Girl Scout catalog for Brownies to color. It was described in the catalog: "Color-Me Daisy Girl Scout Doll. 11942 $13.00. Hours of fun for imaginative girls. Color doll with the nontoxic, water soluble markers (included), play with her, put on a puppet show – then wash her with darks in the washing machine and color her again! 20 inches tall doll in full Daisy Girl Scout uniform. Back pocket with Velcro closure for storing markers. White polyester/cotton with black graphics. Imported."

18" cloth Brownies in black and white versions were available in the 1997/1998 catalog. The dolls are unmarked and have painted features and yarn hair and wear a brown cotton skirt, vest, and blue button-down-the-front short-sleeved blouse. The matching brown beanie hat has a blue Brownie logo. The dolls are official and sold for $27.00 in the catalog. The next year's catalog featured Girl Scout outfits that are currently available.

10" wide velour Girl Scout Bus and Finger Puppets, #11802, has four finger puppets that can be zipped into back of bus, $24.00 retail in 2001/2002 catalog.

Two 11" cloth Daisy dolls with embroidered mouth, black eyes, bright pink yarn ponytails with yellow bands, a sewn-on red scalp wig, striped arms and legs, with blue daisy jumper and shoes and yellow tie around her neck. The black version has black yarn hair with black sewn-on cloth scalp wig. They have an elastic loop on the top of the head so the doll can be hung on the wall. This is an official doll and sold for $7.00.

Two 11" cloth Brownie dolls with embroidered mouth, black eyes, bright orange yarn ponytails with tan bands, a sewn-on orange scalp wig, blue cloth arms, yellow striped legs, brown jumper with blue trim, shoes, and yellow tie around her neck. The black version has black yarn hair with black sewn-on cloth scalp wig. They have an elastic loop on the top of the head so the doll can be hung on the wall. This is an official doll and sold for $7.00.

The first official 17" porcelain Juliette Low doll known as Daisy was made in a limited edition of 450 by artist Elena George. She has porcelain arms and lower legs with a cloth torso. She has molded-on shoes, painted brown eyes, molded and painted hair, and closed mouth and wears a peach ballgown with bustle trimmed with rosettes. Incised on back of breastplate below where the dress starts is "DAISY/Elena George/1997;" some are also signed by hand "Elena George" and the date. She is also marked with the green and white GS insignia on the back. She was priced at $125.00. Their edition sold out and is no longer available through Girl Scout Councils.

The second official 17" porcelain Juliette Low doll, also made by Elena George, is a limited edition of 2,200 and is dressed in a 1919 khaki uniform. She has brown painted eyes, molded and painted brown hair in bun, closed mouth, and molded-on black two-strap shoes. She wears a khaki two-piece uniform with the GS logo trim on the lapels and on her matching brimmed hat. She is numbered, and some are signed on the bottom of the foot. She is also marked with the green and white GS insignia on the back. She is official, priced at $50.00, and is available through the Girl Scout Councils. For more information, write Elena George, Elena Collectibles, P. O. Box 8312, Savannah, GA 31412.

Girl Scout USA Catalog, 1999/2000

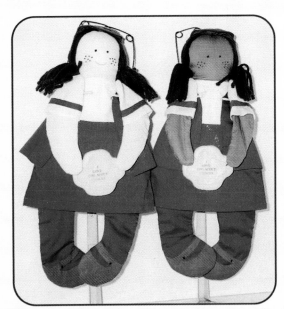

The 1999/2000 catalog shows a 15" cloth wallhanging with a metal hanger. The doll comes in white and black variations and has painted features. She is dressed in a green and white costume and holds a paper cookie that says, "I love Girl Scout Cookies." It is official and priced at $15.00.

Effanbee, 2000 – 2002

Effanbee again was licensed to make official Girl Scout dolls, and they appeared in the 2000/2001 Girl Scout catalog. These are 9" unmarked vinyl dolls, offered in African-American, white, Asian, and Hispanic. The dolls have synthetic long wigs with black or blonde hair, blue or brown set plastic eyes, painted brows, and closed mouths. They also carry the gold paper Effanbee heart tag and come with a white plastic Effanbee marked stand. Effanbee was acquired by the Robert Tonner Doll Company in 2002.

Four 9" vinyl Effanbee Brownie dolls with synthetic long hair in braids, plastic eyes, and closed mouths. They are dressed as ethnic types, African American, white, Asian, and Hispanic. They wear brown skirts with matching vests and beanie caps and have blue short-sleeved blouses with white ribbon ties. They have brown plastic shoes with white socks and come with gold paper heart tags and white plastic marked stands. $25.00.

Four 9" vinyl Effanbee Junior Girl Scout dolls with synthetic long hair, set plastic eyes, and closed mouths. They are dressed as ethnic types, African American, white, Asian, and Hispanic. They wear green skirts with matching vests and brimmed caps and have white short-sleeved blouses with green trim. They have brown plastic shoes with white socks and come with gold paper heart tags and white plastic marked stands. $25.00.

Tent Play Set, 2000 – 2001

This tent set is featured in the 2000/2001 Girl Scout catalog. The cloth dolls are 7½" tall, and the bears are 3" tall. They are official. "Hour of fun, at home or away. Includes 2 dolls with removable outfits, 2 fuzzy teddy bears, 2 nylon sleeping bags, and a tent with zipper and flap closure in front, pretend window in back, and Girl Scout on the side. Soft, packable pieces store inside the tent for fun on the go. Imported." Item #11784. $26.00.

Five wooden nesting dolls marked on bottom "Kasaroua," all dressed in the same Girl Scout uniform, range in height from 1" to 5". Painted features, no price available. *Courtesy Pidd Miller.*

2002

Currently available in some Girl Scout Council Shops are the wooden nesting dolls with painted costumes of Cadette, Junior Girl Scout, Brownie, Daisy, and Trefoil Girl. The set of five nesting dolls ranges in height from 1" to 5" tall, and the set is priced at $24.95. They are marked on the bottom with a gold paper tag that reads "Made in Russia" and printed in white is the word "Savkoyeva." They are called "Matryoshka" in Russia, handpainted, from the Karelia region located in the northwestern part of Russia. Each unique with slight variations.

This 11" all-cloth Juliette Gordon Low was available in 2002 for $12.95 and is tagged on leg "Designed and Manufactured for//Biography Buddies Ltd. by//Yottoy Productions, Inc.//New York, NY 10001 USA//All rights reserved//Handmade in China." She also carries a paper hangtag. Clothes and hat are not removable.

A talented doll artist has made miniature Juliette Low and Scout dolls, including Cadette, Brownie, and Junior Girl Scout in various uniforms. The sizes range from 3½" to 5½". Prices range from $50.00 – 75.00.

6", a one-of-a-kind polymer Brownie doll waving an American flag. Each Brownie is individually sculpted by Elizabeth Cooper. She wears a handsewn brown felt outfit with brown felt Brownie cap and holds an American flag. Doll stand included. Retail $95.00 plus $5.95 S&H.

6" one-of-a-kind polymer Brownie dolls. Each Brownie is individually sculpted by Elizabeth Cooper. This Brownie troop has handsewn brown felt outfits with brown felt Brownie caps and are holding an American flag. Doll stand included. Retail $95.00 plus $5.95 S&H.

Commercially-made Clothing

Girl Scout clothing was made by several different companies though the years, some official and some not. There probably are more Scout uniforms that have not been identified by maker and have not been reported. In the 1920s and 1940s, Glad Togs and Dolly Togs made clothing for dolls like Effanbee's Patsy family and Ideal's Shirley Temple dolls, and this clothing would fit any doll in the range of sizes that they offered. Girl Scout uniforms made by these companies are shown on Patsy Ann and other composition dolls in this book. These uniforms are extremely rare and cost an average of $250.00 up. It is unknown how these outfits were packaged as none has been reported still in its own box.

Terri Lee, circa 1956 – 1963

In 1956, the Girl Scout organization sold through their catalogs uniforms to fit 8" dolls manufactured by Terri Lee. Most of these are marked and came in small fold-up boxes and were on the market for about three years.

Although Terri Lee sold their own Tiny Terri Lee and Ginger dressed as Scouts, there is no record that the 8" doll clothes were sold separately through Terri Lee.

8" hard plastic Ginny doll marked "Vogue® Dolls/© 1986 R. Dakin & Co./Made in China" wearing Terri Lee long-sleeved green cotton uniform with snap button closures down front, green plastic belt, green socks, green plastic shoes, and green felt beanie hat with white GS logo. $75.00 for costume only, mint in box.

Two boxed uniform sets for Terri Lee Girl Scout and Brownie costumes. The brown box for the Brownie reads "8" Brownie Scout Doll//Dress Uniform." The original price, circa 1956 – 1959, was $1.50. The Girl Scout box is green and white, and both boxes have silhouettes of the Girl Scout trefoil logo. $75.00 for costume, mint in box.

Beehler Arts, Ltd. (Kim/Virga), circa 1950s

Beehler Arts, Ltd. appears to be the parent company for Virga and Kim as they each produced dress-up costumes for 8" dolls, using a similar box and the same style number. The uniform is polished green cotton with gold emblem on the hat and collar, and Virga advertised they would fit "any 8" doll."

Box for Kim Dress-Ups to fit any 8" doll is gold and blue and has a cellophane window opening on the top. The bottom of the package reads "Kim" and gives a list of available costumes. The Girl Scout costume is C-133. The address for Kim Dolls is 47 West Street, New York City.

8" hard plastic Virga (Pam or Kim) from the 1950s is a rare black version with black synthetic wig in long braids. She has sleep eyes, closed mouth, and five-piece body. The Girl Scout green polished cotton uniform has a gold emblem on the collar, a dark green belt, gold buckle, a gold ribbon tie, and dark green beanie hat with gold emblem and is not an official costume. Costume alone, mint in box, $125.00; excellent condition without box, $65.00.

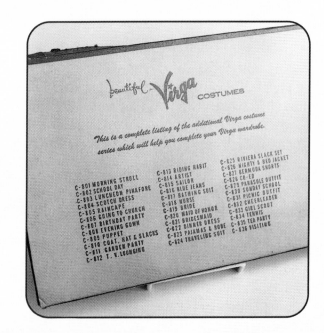

Box for Virga Playthings Dress-Ups also is blue and gold with a cellophane window on the top so you can view the costume. This Virga box contains a mint Girl Scout costume. (See page 58 for doll in costume.) The bottom of the package also gives a list of Virga costumes and the Girl Scout is #C-833. The box also says, "Manufactured by Beehler Arts Ltd., 47 West Street, New York City." leading one to assume Beehler Arts made both Virga and Kim costumes."

8" unmarked hard plastic Virga "Camp Girl" #P-833, with blue sleep eyes, dark hard molded lashes, closed mouth, synthetic cinnamon-colored wig, and bent knees wears a long-sleeved green polished cotton Virga Girl Scout unofficial dress, with white snap button closure, yellow tie, green hat, dark green socks, and black shoes, circa 1958 – 1960. $100.00. *Courtesy Lynne Armstrong.*

Jane Miller, circa 1955 – 1965

During the mid-1950s – mid-1960s, Jane Miller of Lafayette, California, made three sizes of Girl Scout and Brownie uniforms that were sold through department stores. The sizes were to fit 8", 11" and 18" dolls. They were tagged "Jane Miller//Lafayette, Calif." and were green cotton, buttoned down the front, with a dark belt, yellow satin ribbon tie, and dark green hat. These costumes were not official.

8" hard plastic Madame Alexander with black synthetic wig, sleep eyes, closed mouth wears a tagged Jane Miller green long-sleeved Girl Scout costume with snap buttons down the front, yellow cotton tie, green felt attached belt, and dark green hat. $55.00 – 100.00 Girl Scout or Brownie costume.

8" Nancy Ann Storybook hard plastic walker "Muffie" with red tightly curled poodle-cut caracal wig, sleep eyes, closed mouth, and painted brows. She is marked "Storybook//Dolls//California//Muffie." She wears marked Jane Miller costume of tan cotton Brownie uniform with Brownie figure stamped on bodice pocket, dark brown snap closures on front of bodice, and belt of same tan fabric with dark brown button closure. She wears white rayon socks with brown vinyl shoes. Her dark brown hat is four-piece older wool felt with no elastic at chin. The costume is marked with a white ribbon embroidered with black thread that reads "Jane Miller//Lafayette Calif." $250.00.

18" Effanbee hard plastic Honey with synthetic wig, sleep eyes, and closed mouth wears a Jane Miller Girl Scout uniform tagged "Jane Miller//Lafayette, Calif." The uniform is long-sleeved, has cuffs, dark green buttons down the front, a dark green felt belt, yellow ribbon satin tie, and dark green hat. $75.00 – 100.00.

11" hard plastic Nancy Ann Storybook "Debbie" with synthetic long red braids, tagged Jane Miller Girl Scout costume, with long sleeves, snap buttons down the front, dark green felt belt, yellow cotton tie with green insignia, white socks, and black shoes. Uniform, $75.00 – 100.00. Courtesy Lynne Armstrong.

Premier Doll Togs, Inc., circa 1950s – 1980s

Premier Doll Togs, Inc., New York, sold Girl Scout and Brownie uniforms to fit several sizes of dolls during the 1950s. They ranged from 8", 11", 15", and larger, and they were made to fit both slim and chubby dolls including Madame Alexander, Cosmopolitan Ginger, Vogue Ginny, and Wee Imp. The Girl Scout dress is long-sleeved with snap button closure, dark green felt belt, yellow cotton tie, and dark green hat. The Brownie uniform has short sleeves, brown snaps on the bodice, a Brownie logo on the bodice pocket, and a dark brown hat with a decorative seam around the bottom. These are not official.

8" hard plastic Madame Alexander wears a Premier long-sleeved Girl Scout uniform with dark green snap closures, yellow tie, and green hat shown with an unopened costume in Premier labeled bag. Mint in package uniforms are $100.00.

8" hard plastic Cosmopolitan Ginger wears brown short-sleeved Brownie uniform with snap closures on the bodice, a patch pocket on the bodice with a Brownie logo, brown socks, black shoes, and a dark brown hat.

Progressive Doll Outfits, circa 1950s – 1960

Progressive Doll Outfits were also sold in the 1950s and 1960s. These were packaged in a pink and blue cardboard box with see-through top and blue graphics. The long-sleeved Girl Scout dress was made of green cotton with collar, three white buttons down the front, a patch pocket on the skirt, and matching fabric belt with white button closure. There was a matching hat in the same green fabric. These costumes were made to fit slim and chubby dolls from 9" to 16". Only Girl Scout uniforms have been found, and some came with matching panties. These uniforms are not official.

Mint in box Progressive long-sleeved green cotton uniform with white buttons, patch pocket on skirt, and matching green fabric belt and hat. $125.00.

14" hard plastic Mary Hoyer with red synthetic wig, sleep eyes, closed mouth, and five-piece slim-style body wears a Progressive Doll Outfit Girl Scout costume with white button closure, yellow tie, and green matching belt and hat with yellow trim. Mint in box costume alone, $125.00.

11" vinyl Effanbee Fluffy wears a Progressive Doll Outfit Girl Scout costume with yellow tie, green belt, and green hat with yellow trim. Mint in box costume alone, $125.00.

16" hard plastic Ideal Posey wears a Progressive Doll Outfit Girl Scout costume with white button closure, yellow tie, and green matching belt and hat with yellow trim. Mint in box costume alone, $125.00.

Cosmopolitan Doll and Toy Corp.

Cosmopolitan Doll and Toy Corp. put out their own Ginger doll dressed as a Brownie. These uniforms are tagged "Fashions for Ginger//Cosmopolitan Doll & Toy Corp.//Jackson Heights, N.Y.//Trade Mark." They came with hat, belt, and dress, matching panties, socks, and shoes. One catalog shows the Brownie uniform with yellow socks instead of the usual brown. The costumes were not officially licensed, however.

Cosmopolitan "Fashions for Ginger" red box with gold striped top and see-through cellophane window holds a complete Ginger Brownie uniform. $125.00.

8" hard plastic Cosmopolitan Ginger with synthetic brunette wig, sleep eyes, and closed mouth wears a tagged Cosmopolitan "Fashions for Ginger" Brownie short-sleeved brown cotton dress with brown snap front closures, brown vinyl belt, dark brown shoes, socks, and hat. She carries a brown purse inscribed in white, "Ginger." Dressed Ginger, $225.00; mint in package Brownie uniform, $125.00.

8" hard plastic Cosmopolitan Ginger with synthetic blonde wig, sleep eyes, and closed mouth wears a tagged Cosmopolitan "Fashions for Ginger" short-sleeved brown cotton dress with brown snap front closures, brown vinyl belt, dark brown shoes, yellow socks, and dark brown replaced hat. She carries a brown purse inscribed in white, "Ginger." Dressed Ginger, $225.00; mint in package Brownie uniform, $125.00.

Photocopy of original Cosmopolitan Ginger catalog shows the Brownie costume, #331 in the Novelty Series. *Courtesy Carolyn Nestrick.*

8" hard plastic Cosmopolitan Ginger with synthetic blonde wig, sleep eyes, and closed mouth wears a tagged Cosmopolitan "Fashions for Ginger" short-sleeved brown cotton dress with brown snap front closures, brown vinyl belt, dark brown shoes, yellow socks, and dark brown hat. Dressed Ginger, $225.00; mint in package Brownie uniform, $125.00.

Effanbee, 1965 – 1974

In 1965, Effanbee came out with their vinyl Fluffy as a Brownie and a Junior Girl Scout. They also sold the Girl Scout and Brownie outfits for 8" dolls. These outfits are not tagged. They did come in a marked boxes, green for Girl Scouts, brown for Brownies. They were available through 1974 when they were offered at sale prices. During this time, Effanbee also made a swimsuit and shorts set for both Brownie and Girl Scout. These were sold in packages and could only be bought as outfits. These costumes are hard to find.

Effanbee Girl Scout green cotton costume to fit an 8" doll with yellow ribbon tie, green plastic belt, dark green hat with white trefoil logo in dark green box marked, "GIRL(GS®) SCOUTS" in white lettering with see-through plastic cover. Price in box, $100.00.

Effanbee Girl Scout set of green shorts and white cotton blouse with "GS" stamped in green on the pocket to fit 8" dolls. Packaged in clear cellophane bag with dark green cardboard top in white, "GIRL (GS) SCOUTS//8" Girl Scout Doll Camp Uniform." Price in package, $50.00 – 75.00.

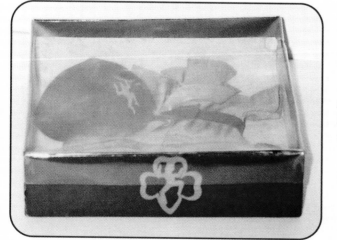

Effanbee Brownie costume in hard-to-find brown box marked with the Girl Scout trefoil logo, $95.00.

Unknown Makers

These 8" hard plastic dolls show a variety of factory-made Girl Scout and Brownie uniforms by an unknown maker. Prices would vary if the doll is included or if the uniform was a put-together.

Unusual ones like the 8" Madame Alexander Brownie with round buttons would be more. These uniforms are not official.

8" vinyl Madame Alexander doll models an unusual tan short-sleeved cotton commercially-made Brownie costume with round ball-type buttons by unknown maker.

8" hard plastic doll models a green short-sleeved Girl Scout uniform by unknown maker with dark green snaps down front, dark green plastic belt with gold buckle, and dark green felt replacement Terri Lee cap.

8" hard plastic doll models tan Brownie shorts with white blouse, possibly made by Effanbee, with brown stamped Girl Scout logo on bodice.

103

8" hard plastic Madame Alexander doll with strawberry blonde wig in ponytails models a tan short-sleeved cotton Brownie uniform by unknown maker with dark brown snaps down the front, and brown plastic belt with gold buckle. She wears a dark brown cap.

An unmarked 8" vinyl doll models a green long-sleeved Girl Scout uniform by unknown maker with dark green vinyl belt and gold buckle. She has an added brimmed hat trimmed with green grosgrain ribbon, resembling a Leader's hat of the 1950s.

8" vinyl Madame Alexander doll with brown hair and eyes, wears a short- sleeved tan Brownie dress by unknown maker with two dark brown snaps closing the front, a vinyl dark brown belt with yellow plastic buckle, and a collar with white top stitching. There is a pocket on the upper bodice, and she wears a dark brown cap.

Home-made Costumes

Creative doll costumers have shown their originality and talent in dressing many dolls in Girl Scout and Brownie uniforms in addition to the officially dressed Girl Scout and Brownie dolls sanctioned by the Girl Scout organization. Using material from old uniforms, found at flea markets, doll shows, and garage sales, a good seamstress can give an authentic look to her favorite doll.

Pidd Miller, a Girl Scout collector, created a costume for a 10" composition unmarked doll with painted blue side-glancing eyes, mohair wig, and closed mouth. Using scraps of official 1928 material, she made a long-sleeved green Girl Scout uniform in the 1928 style.

21" painted hard plastic Effanbee Honey with red synthetic wig, sleep eyes, and closed mouth from the late 1940s, dressed in a dark blue old serge material two-piece Mariner's costume with two white bands around the wrist. She wears a matching dark blue hat.

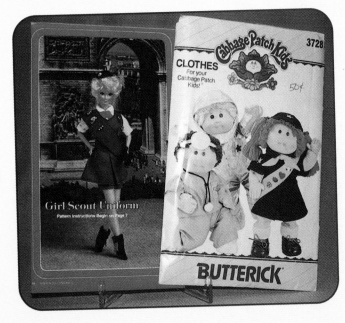

Newer commercial patterns are available for 11½" fashion dolls like Barbie, and Butterick has uniform patterns to fit Cabbage Patch Kids. Courtesy Lynne Armstrong.

14" hard plastic Arranbee Nanette, with brunette wig, sleep eyes, and closed mouth, dressed in short-sleeved brown uniform in old Brownie fabric with buttons on bodice, brown belt, and matching brown hat with orange emblem, and a 15" hard plastic American Character Sweet Sue with reddish blonde synthetic wig, sleep eyes, and closed mouth, dressed in Girl Scout uniform in old green fabric with button front closing, dark green belt, and dark green hat. She wears a red tie.

This 14" Georgene Novelties cloth doll with mask face, blonde curly wig, and painted features has been re-dressed as an early Girl Scout in khaki camp outfit. The heavy felt hat has an early Girl Scout button pinned to it. The button and the costume reflect the 1918 – 1928 era. $125.00.

8" hard plastic American Character Betsy McCall, circa 1957 – 1963, with synthetic wig rooted to a plastic skull cap, sleep eyes, closed mouth and body with jointed knees, wears a brown homemade Brownie costume with dark brown plastic belt, dark brown hat, original black plastic shoes, and white socks. Dressed doll, $125.00.

15" hard plastic doll by unknown maker has dark blonde synthetic wig, sleep eyes, and closed mouth, and wears a homemade hat and a Georgene Novelties outfit cut down to fit her. Doll, $75.00. Courtesy Nancy Nunn.

16" composition Effanbee Patsy Joan with molded painted hair, sleep eyes, and closed mouth is dressed in a homemade dress to represent the Girl Scout of the 1930s.

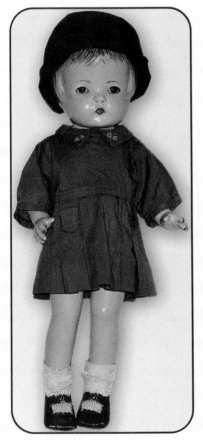

15" hard plastic Ideal Saucy Walker with red synthetic braids, blue sleep eyes with eye shadow, and open mouth with two upper teeth wears a homemade Senior Girl Scout uniform of the late 1950s, $125.00.

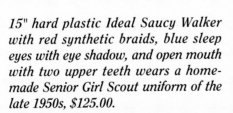

Marked "R & B" (Arranbee) hard plastic doll with red synthetic wig wears a long-sleeved Georgene Novelties Girl Scout uniform with red tie, altered to fit this doll, with a dark green felt hat.

A small cloth doll made by a Scout's mother uses the official Girl Scout blue, green, and white print fabric for the blouse, and a green bonnet, vest, and long skirt. This is a novel keepsake with all of the girls' names embroidered on the skirt.

8" hard plastic Dress Me doll with painted eyes, blonde mohair wig, and closed mouth, in homemade long-sleeved Girl Scout uniform with buttons down the front, yellow tie, and dark green hat with white GS logo.

8" hard plastic Dress Me doll with painted eyes, mohair wig, and closed mouth in homemade short-sleeved Brownie uniform with white blouse, dark brown skirt, sash, and hat. She has molded-on white shoes with bows.

8" hard plastic Dress Me doll with reddish blonde wig, sleep eyes, closed mouth, and painted-on shoes wears a home-made Senior Girl Scout uniform of green, short-sleeved blouse with medium green sash, dark green skirt, and matching hat. $25.00. *Courtesy Carolyn Nestrick.*

15" cloth Brownie doll with painted features, made by doll artist Joyce Patterson. The doll wears a brown and white striped shirt, dark brown jumper, sash with badges, and dark tennis shoes. $300.00. Photo courtesy Pidd Miller.

15" cloth Girl Scout doll with painted features, made by doll artist Joyce Patterson. The doll wears a green striped shirt, dark green skirt, and sash with badges. She holds two small dolls. $300.00. Photo courtesy Pidd Miller.

15" vinyl Fisher Price doll with decal eyes, short synthetic wig, and closed smiling mouth wears a homemade Brownie uniform made by Diane Miller with brown and white patterned short-sleeved blouse with orange tie, dark brown jumper, and dark brown Girl Scout hat with orange logo. Courtesy Pidd Miller.

Cloth homemade doll by Karen Ramey from 1989 wears a Girl Scout Leader's costume with striped blouse and dark skirt and hat. Ramey was the leader of the first Girl Scout troop to earn the Girl Scout Doll Collector patch. Courtesy Pidd Miller.

14" homemade cloth doll with short yarn wig, painted brown eyes, and closed mouth wears a brown and white shirt, tan, short overalls, and dark brown hat with orange Brownie logo like a Brownie from the 1970s.

8" unmarked cloth doll has painted features and wears a homemade Girl Scout outfit that is pinned on, dark felt hat with white Girl Scout logo, painted brown shoes, and white socks are sewn on as part of the feet. $35.00.

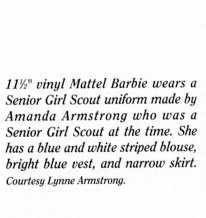

11½" vinyl Mattel Barbie wears a Senior Girl Scout uniform made by Amanda Armstrong who was a Senior Girl Scout at the time. She has a blue and white striped blouse, bright blue vest, and narrow skirt. Courtesy Lynne Armstrong.

Camp Fire Girls and Blue Birds

In 1910, when the Boy Scouts became a formal organization, the question was asked, "What about the girls?" Among a group of "idea people" interested in the welfare of the girls was Dr. Luther Halsey Gulick and his wife, Charlotte Vetter Gulick. Dr. Gulick helped get things underway during the summer of 1910. The program started with a special American touch of Indian lore and still keeps its own identifying symbolism — thus the Camp Fire Girls are older than the Girl Scouts that were started in 1912.

The Gulicks had six children of their own, four girls and two boys, and were authorities on child health, recreation, and education. They founded the organization to give teenage girls a chance to enjoy outdoor activities. The original Council Fire costume, circa 1920, looked like an Indian dress with fringe around the skirt and neck and beaded decorations. Former Congresswoman and child film star Shirley Temple Black was a Camp Fire Girl.

Dr. Gulick was associated with the YMCA from 1890 to 1911. He worked with William Langdon, Ernest Seton, and Daniel Beard helping to form and promote the Boy Scouts organization.

In 1910, Charlotte Gulick formed a girls' summer camp in Maine. Charlotte decided that Indian lore and traditions would give interest to her camp that she called "WoHeLo," the name taken from the first two letters of the words, "work, health, and love." William Langdon and his wife created a pageant with "Camp Fire Girls" in Thetford, Vermont. The Langdons and the Gulicks collaborated about forming a national organization for girls.

On April 10, 1911, James West of the Boy Scout organization issued a press release telling that a national society for girls like the Boy Scouts was being organized and it would be called Camp Fire Girls of America. Until his retirement in 1940, West maintained that the Camp Fire Girls was the sister organization of the Boy Scouts.

In 1914, Dr. Charles Eastman, a Sioux Indian named Ohiyesa, wrote a book, *Indian Scout Talks: A Guide for Boy Scouts and Camp Fire Girls.* In this book he gives ceremonies, symbols, words, and names appropriate for these young people's organizations.

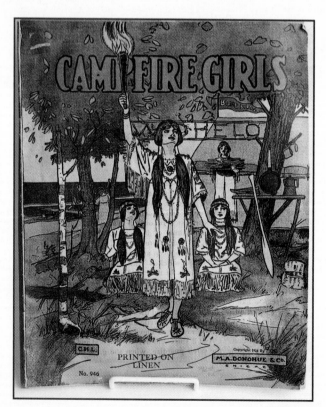

Camp Fire Girls is a story about camp and the adventures the girls have that summer. It is printed on linen and was copyrighted in 1916 by M. A. Donohue & Co.

HOLIDAY GIFT SUGGESTIONS

60—Harmar—She is a real Camp Fire Girl with a khaki ceremonial gown trimmed with leather fringe, a necklace of beads, a headband and moccasins. Her head and hands are of very hard composition. Body and limbs are stuffed. Her complexion is of Indian type. Legs and arms turn easily and she sits and stands comfortably. When standing she is 13 inches high.
Price, carrying charge prepaid.. **$1.25**

60A—Lodorbes — A Camp Fire Girl, the big sister of Harmar; Lodorbes, the big sister, is dressed and made in the same way as Harmar, but is a much larger girl. She stands 29½ in. high. Dressed as you see her, carrying charges prepaid_____ **$2.98**

61 — Little Indian Brave — Wears khaki suit trimmed with leather fringe, moccasins and a bright colored feather; arms and head of composition; body and limbs stuffed; arms and legs adjustable to any angle; stands 13 inches high. Dressed as you see him; carrying charges prepaid _____ **$1.25**

61A — Big Indian Brave — The great big brother of Little Indian Brave— an exact counterpart except that he **stands 30 inches high.** He is a very big boy **as you will** understand. Dressed like Little Indian Brave, carrying charges prepaid_____ **$2.98**

1924 advertisement from The Camp Fire Outfitting Co., 199 Greene Street, New York City, shows, "Harmar, a real Camp Fire Girl with khaki ceremonial gown trimmed with leather fringe, a necklace of beads, a headband, and moccasins. Her head and hands are of very hard composition. Body and limbs are stuffed. Her complexion is of Indian type. Legs and arms turn easily and she sits and stands comfortably. When standing, she is 13" high." This doll costs $1.25. It also describes Lodorbes, big sister of Harmar, who is 29½" high and dressed as you see her. This doll costs $2.98.

Founded in 1910, Camp Fire Girls was incorporated in 1912. The organization existed as Camp Fire Girls into the 1970s when the Camp Fire Girls became co-ed and was then known as Camp Fire, and later as Camp Fire Boys and Girls. The youngest members of the Camp Fire Girls were known as Blue Birds, and the Blue Bird program was officially started in 1913. The first Camp Fire Council was formed in 1918 in Kansas City, Missouri. In 1962, Junior Hi level was formed, later to became Discovery when boys are admitted to the organization in 1975. In 1983, kindergarteners were known as Sparks but combined with Blue Birds in 1989. A new program for kindergarten, first and second graders was started which was called Starflight. A book on the history of the Camp Fire organization, *Wo-He-Lo: The Camp Fire History,* was published in 1980 by Camp Fire, Inc.

26" plastic Georgene Novelties Blue Bird with painted side-glancing blue eyes, painted lashes and eyebrows, closed pouty mouth, red accents at nostrils, yellow yarn wig in braids, and cloth body. She wears a Blue Bird navy cap, white blouse, blue skirt, and red vest. A Blue Bird pin has been added to her cap. Circa 1950s, $250.00.

28" Georgene Novelties cloth Camp Fire Girl with painted features and mask face, yellow yarn braids, wearing an original Camp Fire Girl's hat cut down to fit her, original white blouse with red tie, dark blue skirt, and panties with replaced shoes and socks. Circa 1940s – 1950s, $100.00.

The Terri Lee Company made a 16" hard plastic Blue Bird Terri Lee and Camp Fire Girl, circa 1946 – 1962. These official uniforms are tagged Terri Lee. The 10" Tiny Terry Lee, circa 1955 – 1960, also was made as a Camp Fire Girl or Blue Bird, and these official costumes are also tagged Terri Lee.

Early paper hangtag for Camp Fire Girls costume.

16" hard plastic Terri Lee with painted eyes, lashes, and brows, closed red pouty lips, and blonde wig wears a Blue Bird uniform of blue skirt, white blouse, red vest, and blue cap. A Blue Bird silhouette in paler blue is on the cap and skirt. She has saddle oxfords and white stockings. Circa 1946 – 1962, $500.00 – 700.00.

16" hard plastic Terri Lee with painted eyes, lashes, and brows, closed red pouty lips, and brunette wig wears a Camp Fire Girl uniform of blue skirt, white blouse with red tie, and blue cap. She has saddle oxfords and white stockings. Circa 1946 – 1962, $500.00 – 700.00.

10" hard plastic Tiny Terri Lee Camp Fire Girl with synthetic dark blonde wig, sleep eyes, extra long eyelashes, and painted features wears a white blouse with red tie, navy blue skirt and cap, saddle oxfords, and white socks, and is from the 1955 – 1960 era, $250.00.

10" hard plastic Tiny Terri Lee Blue Bird with synthetic brunette wig, sleep eyes, extra long eyelashes, and painted features wears a white blouse with red vest, navy blue skirt, and cap with a pale blue bird silhouette. She has saddle oxfords and white socks and is from the 1955 – 1960 era, $250.00.

8" vinyl Nancy Drew doll in ceremonial Indian Camp Fire Girl's outfit. Made by unknown maker, she is marked "Hong Kong" on the head and back. She has synthetic yellow braids with a blue and white print headband and matching trim on skirt, sleep eyes, and closed mouth. It is not official, possibly circa 1970s. Book, $25.00; doll, $30.00.

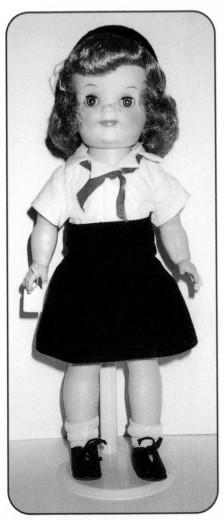

15" vinyl Effanbee Patsy Ann Camp Fire Girl with blue sleep eyes, freckles across face, and synthetic wig. She wears a dark blue skirt, white blouse with red ribbon tie, navy blue cap, black shoes, and white stockings. Patsy Ann in vinyl was originally produced in 1959. $250.00+.

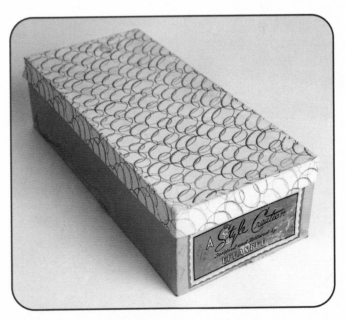

Effanbee box for Blue Bird or Camp Fire Girl Doll has pink circle shell pattern lid; blue label at end of box.

117

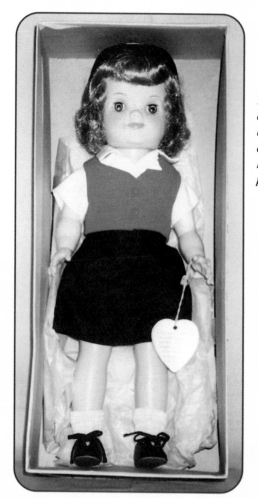

15" vinyl Effanbee Patsy Ann Blue Bird with blue sleep eyes, freckles across face, and synthetic wig. She wears a dark blue skirt, white blouse with red vest, navy blue cap, black shoes, white stockings, and has her original box. She carries the gold paper heart wrist tag Effanbee used on many of its dolls. Patsy Ann in vinyl was originally produced in 1959. $250.00+.

Pair of 16" vinyl Effanbee Suzettes who have the slimmer body of a teenager. They each have a dark blonde synthetic wig, blue sleep eyes, and wore a blue skirt, white blouse, and red vest as a Blue Bird or white shirt and red tie as a Camp Fire Girl. Both wear navy blue caps and have white socks and black shoes. Suzette was made in 1959 and was offered for several years. Relatively difficult to find, $250.00+.

8" vinyl Effanbee Fluffy Camp Fire Girl with synthetic wig, sleep eyes, and closed mouth. She wears a dark blue skirt, white blouse, and blue cap. She is missing her red ribbon tie, but does have her original red box. Circa 1965 and later, $75.00 – 100.00.

8" black vinyl Effanbee Fluffy Blue Bird with synthetic wig, sleep eyes, and closed mouth. She wears a dark blue skirt, red vest, white blouse, and blue cap with white bird logo. Circa 1965 and later, $75.00 – 100.00.

8" black vinyl Effanbee Fluffy Camp Fire Girl with synthetic wig, sleep eyes, and closed mouth. She wears a dark blue skirt, white blouse with red tie, and blue cap. Circa 1965 and later, $75.00 – 100.00.

119

11" vinyl Effanbee Fluffy Blue Bird with synthetic wig, sleep eyes, and closed mouth. She wears a dark blue skirt, red vest, white blouse, and blue cap with white bird. She carries the gold paper heart Effanbee paper tag. The 11" size is harder to find. Circa 1965 and later. $75.00 – 200.00.

11" vinyl Effanbee Fluffy Camp Fire Girl with synthetic wig, sleep eyes, and closed mouth. She wears a dark blue skirt, white blouse with red ribbon tie, and blue cap. The 11" size is harder to find. Circa 1965 and later. $75.00 – 200.00.

Two 8" vinyl Effanbee Fluffy Blue Birds with dark blue box and slight wardrobe variations. The one-piece costume at right has gold buttons instead of red on her vest, circa 1965. $75.00 – 100.00.

International Girl Guides and Girl Scouts

Norah Wellings

Norah Wellings, was born in Arleston, England, in 1893 and went to work for cloth doll-maker Chad Valley Company in Wellington in 1919 as a designer. In 1926, she started her own company and began making cloth dolls and toys. She patented a cloth molded face doll head that could have either set or movable eyes and made dolls ranging in size from 7½" to 36" tall. Many of her dolls have side-glancing eyes, and the embroidered labels read "MADE IN ENGLAND//BY//NORAH WELLINGS."

An example of a 10" Norah Wellings Girl Guide from the 1930s has cloth face with painted side-glancing eyes, painted hair, closed mouth, stitched fingers on her cloth hands and wears a dark blue two-piece uniform with red tie and trim on her hat. $250.00. Courtesy Pidd Miller.

Commercially-made by unknown maker, a knitted 12" Brownie doll with embroidered and felt features, yellow yarn hair, brown dress, knitted hat and shoes. Made in England, $45.00. Courtesy Nancy Nunn.

Amanda Jane

The Amanda Jane Company began in England in 1952, selling accessories and costumes to leading London department stores. Amanda Jane was first made in hard plastic in 1958 and called Jinx, but in the 1960s the company produced dress-me dolls with a wide range of packaged wardrobes. The costumes carried a cloth "Amanda Jane" label, and the company began making a vinyl version in 1966. She is marked on her back "MADE IN ENGLAND//Amanda//Jane." The Brownie outfit was described as a brown dress with Brownie insignia and a brown knitted pull-on hat typical of the Brownies' uniform.

7½" vinyl Amanda Jane has side-glancing painted brown eyes, blonde synthetic wig, pale color closed mouth, and a one-piece short-sleeved brown dress with brown vinyl belt and yellow tie, brown pull-on knitted hat, brown stockings and shoes. She carries a brown school bag.

Amanda Jane's Brownie costume could be purchased separately on a card with see-through front. Circa 1970s, dressed doll, $40.00; clothing pack, $25.00.

Peggy Nisbet

Peggy Nisbet began making dolls in 1953 with a coronation figure of Queen Elizabeth. The limited editions of 250 were sold quickly at Harrods, and she soon organized Peggy Nisbet Limited to make dolls of royalty and historical figures. One of those figures was of Olave, Lady Baden-Powell, wife of Lord Baden-Powell, the founder of the Boy Scouts. Agnes, sister of Lord Baden-Powell, established the Girl Guides and Powell's wife, Olave, headed up the organization. The Powells were good friends of Juliette Low who brought the idea of Girl Guides to the United States. The Nisbet company closed their business in the 1990s.

8" hard plastic Peggy Nisbet Lady Baden-Powell, with white wig, painted blue eyes, closed mouth, and painted-on shoes. She wears a two-piece dark blue suit, white blouse with blue tie, and light blue hat with black headband. She carries a black and white paper tag that reads, "Costume//Dolls//by// Peggy//Nisbet//MADE IN ENGLAND." Doll only, $250.00.

8½" hard plastic Peggy Nisbet Lord Baden-Powell, with painted eyes, closed mouth, and painted-on shoes. He wears a khaki shirt and shorts with brown hat, tan knee socks, and brown shoes. The clothes are not removable. His hangtag reads, "A Peggy Nisbet Model//P827//Lord Baden-Powell//Made in England." His box is a reddish color with gold pattern that reads: "PEGGY NISBET DOLLS." $250.00.

Regal Toy Company, 1959 – 1984

Frank Samuels' Regal Toy Company was located in Toronto, Canada, and they made vinyl dolls with hard plastic bodies. Regal's Canadian Brownie Guide is shown on page 124.

Götz, 1964+

Swiss artist Sasha Morgenthaler began making dolls in the 1940s, and her early Sasha dolls are unique with facial painting, clothing, and hand-tied wigs. In 1964, Morgenthaler had the German Götz firm make 16" vinyl dolls for her. In 1965, Frito Ltd. in England also manufactured dolls with Götz for a number of years. In 1994 Götz was again given the license to manufacture Sasha dolls, and one of the dolls they produced was their version of an English Girl Guide (shown on page 124).

13" vinyl Regal Toy "Gail" Canadian Brownie Guide with rooted brunette wig, blue sleep eyes, closed mouth, hard plastic body, a rust dress with dark brown belt, collar and hat, all original with hangtag, circa early 1960s. $30.00. *Courtesy Lynne Armstrong.*

16½" vinyl Götz Puppenfabrik version of English Girl Guide, "Alice," has painted features and synthetic blonde hair in braids. She is marked on the neck "Sasha//;Gotz 94//306" and on her back in a round circle "Sasha//Serie." She wears a blue shirt with orange tie, brown hat, dark blue skirt, knee socks, and black shoes. She carries a wooden staff with black and white flag. She has a brown purse, black belt, and the blue, red and white Sasha tag attached with elastic cord to her waist, circa 1999, $200.00.

Philippines

12½" handmade cloth Girl Scout made in Manila, Philippines as a fund-raiser for Girl Scouts. She wears a green one-piece dress with printed Girl Scout logo, matching sash, and yellow tie. The doll has painted features, black yarn hair, and a straw hat, $43.00. *Courtesy Lynne Armstrong.*

Joy Belle

Logo for the Joy Belles is a green and white oval with a drawing of a daisy that reads: "Joy//Belles//WE SERVE JOYFULLY."

The North Georgia Church of God of Atlanta, Georgia has a Joy Belles program for girls ages, nine to twelve. Their motto: "We Serve Joyfully." Their flower is a daisy, and the colors are yellow, green, and white. Their purpose: "To encourage spiritual growth in the junior girls. To provide opportunities to develop her pearl ability and skill. To help her find a place of service. To provide her with wholesome fellowship and recreation." Joy Belles can earn badges much like the Girl Scouts and also have a travel doll program. Their logo is a green and white oval. A program for girls in grades one to three is called "Blue Belles."

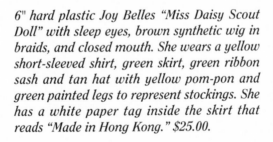

6" hard plastic Joy Belles "Miss Daisy Scout Doll" with sleep eyes, brown synthetic wig in braids, and closed mouth. She wears a yellow short-sleeved shirt, green skirt, green ribbon sash and tan hat with yellow pom-pon and green painted legs to represent stockings. She has a white paper tag inside the skirt that reads "Made in Hong Kong." $25.00.

Surprise Marketing

8" vinyl Surprise Marketing, Ltd. Brownie Guide Doll comes in clear plastic box and is tagged "THE BROWNIE GUIDE DOLL//Approved by the Girl Guide Association//Not recommended for children under three years of age//Surprise Marketing, Ltd. Reading RGA4, U.K. //Sm 1001//CE//Made in China." The doll has a synthetic wig, painted features, pale pink closed lips, and a brown long-sleeved dress with dark brown belt, knitted hat, and a yellow tie. Circa 1980s – 1990s, Surprise Marketing was present at the Toy Fair in New York in 2001. $55.00.

Eden, LLC.

Madeline was available as an 8" hard vinyl doll with painted features, synthetic hair, and jointed body, and also as a 16" cloth doll with yarn hair. Madeline is a literary character created in 1939 by Ludwig Bemelmans. Madeline dolls were manufac- tured from 1992 until mid-2001 by Eden, LLC. Madeline dolls manufactured after March of 2001 may show Eden as the manufacturer since production was taken over by Learning Curve International.

8" vinyl Madeline as a French Scout, with synthetic red hair, closed smiling mouth, painted eyes, button nose, tan shirt, green shorts and matching hat, red tie, and socks, retails for $12.95; accessories, $10.00.

15" all-cloth dressable Madeline has red yarn hair, embroidered features, tan shirt, brown shorts, red tie and socks, and brown shoes. $24.95.

Canadian Girl Guides

Two 10" cloth Girl Guides of Canada with embroidered features and yarn hair. Came also as a black Girl Guide. The Sharpes Brownie wears a short-sleeved dark brown uniform with orange tie, orange and brown belt, and brown shorts. The Girl Guide has a similar uniform in blue with white tie and red and blue belt. Currently available, the doll is priced at $8.00 and the costume is $4.00.

Two 10" cloth Girl Guides of Canada with embroidered features and yarn hair. Came also as a black Girl Guide. The Sharpes Brownie wears a pink sweatsuit uniform that reads, "I promise to share and be a friend" with the Girl Guide logo. The Girl Guide has a similar uniform in dark blue with white maple leaf logo. Additional sweatsuits are available in dark brown and medium blue. Currently available, the doll is priced at $8.00, and the costume is $4.00.

A set of wooden Girl Guide nesting dolls from Canada that include the Leader, Teenager, Girl Guide, Brownie, and pink Sharpes. They range in size from 5½" to 1¾". The small Sharpes says, "I promise to share and be a friend." $15.00 for the set.

8" vinyl Effanbee marked "Fluffy" with molded painted hair, sleep eyes, and closed mouth is dressed as a Girl Guide in long-sleeved light blue blouse, dark blue skirt, dark blue tie and matching hat. She wears blue stockings and white vinyl shoes, $30.00.

Three 10" homemade cloth dolls with painted features and yarn wigs represent Denmark in dark blue long-sleeved dress and cap; Greece in light tan dress; and unknown country in dark brown. $25.00 each.

7" unmarked rigid plastic Girl Scout has painted side-glancing eyes, closed mouth, painted lashes, and molded hair. She is dressed in homemade long-sleeved tan cotton uniform to represent an unidentified country, $30.00.

8" vinyl Girl Guide Brownie with painted side-glancing eyes, pale pink closed mouth, and rooted synthetic hair. From circa 1986 when Girl Guides updated their uniforms. The Brownie see-through yellow and green box shows Brownie inside and includes two other outfits. Separate wardrobe was also available. *Courtesy Pidd Miller.*

Figurines

" Betsy McCall porcelain figurine manufactured by the Heirloom Tradition of Long Beach, California, a collectible division of Tomy Corporation, was available circa 1984 – 1986. The Girl Scout was issued in March, one of a set of 12 figurines representing the months of the year. The figure portrays a Girl Scout in green short-sleeved dress with dark green sash, green hat, green socks, and black shoes. She is mounted on a base that reads on the bottom, "Betsy McCall//Junior Girl Scout//March 1965//©1984 The McCall Publishing Company, all rights reserved." The box comes with a certificate of authenticity and is numbered and signed by the president of McCall Publishing Company. A gift tag is enclosed with registration certification. This is an official doll. $125.00.

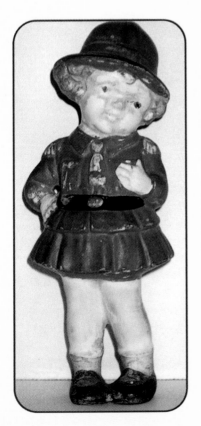

6½" bisque Brownie figurine with molded hat and painted features wears a two-piece brown long-sleeved dress with tie, yellow painted socks, and molded painted black shoes. The Brownie figurine is marked on the back, "Made in Japan" and may be circa 1930s. It is not official. $25.00.

Four figurines of Scouts include a 5" bisque girl in green dress with yellow scarf and shoes; a 6½" Made in Japan bisque girl with tan dress and hat; a 5" porcelain Made in Japan girl in green dress and hat, yellow scarf, and white collar; and a 5" porcelain girl in tan dress and hat with white collar. Each, $25.00 – 50.00. Courtesy Carolyn Nestrick.

5" porcelain Girl Scout figurine marked "Made in Japan" portrays a girl with painted eyes and brows, closed mouth, molded dark blonde hair, green long-sleeved dress with buttons down the front, belt, tan tie, and white collar. She wears blue and white socks and black molded-on shoes. She has on a green hat and looks like she may also have a backpack. $50.00. Courtesy Lynne Armstrong.

Two 3" porcelain bear figurines made in 1995 by Lucy Rigg for ENESCO. They are marked "Lucy and Me//©1995//Lucy Rigg, Licensee//ENESCO//Made in China." The Junior Girl Scout and Brownie are selling cookies. Unknown if officially licensed. $15.00.

7" porcelain figurine of Girl Scout with umbrella was probably homemade. It is marked "Calder" on the bottom and shows a girl with blonde molded and painted hair wearing a short-sleeved green dress with yellow tie and matching green cap with the initials "GS". Not official, $5.00.

4" porcelain Royal Doulton Bunnykins dressed as a Brownie in brown long-sleeved dress with tie and molded-on hat was issued by Royal Doulton from 1987 to 1993. Designed by Graham Tongue, modeled by Warren Platt, the back is stamped BK5, $125.00.
Courtesy Pidd Miller.

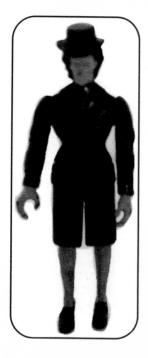

3¾" hard plastic Playskool Girl Scout Leader. $35.00. Courtesy Pidd Miller.

3" pewter Brownie figurine with molded-on hat and uniform with sash is marked "© R.B. '87." $25.00.

3½" pewter Girl Scout with molded-on hat and uniform is marked "© R-B 500" and on the back of the right heel, "1988 RB." $25.00.

6" and 8" metal Girl Scout figurines with oxidized copper finish were sculpted by Marjorie Daingerfield. These are official and were shown in the Girl Scout catalogs from 1955 until 1966/1967. A plate on the front of the figurine allowed them to be engraved. $45.00 – 75.00.

Two 2¼" lead figures, a Girl Scout, #38, offered in catalog 1926 – 1932; and a Girl Guide, 1927 – 1939. This was a single figure in 1927 in the Civilian Series and presented again in 1934 in boxed set of eight Girl Guides. They both wear the same type uniform with long skirts, black ties, and wide brimmed hats, $80.00 – 100.00 each. *Courtesy Lynne Armstrong.*

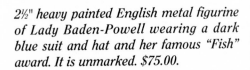

The 1988/1989 Girl Scout catalog offered a 2½" pewter plate figurine of Juliette Low. It is marked "JULIETTE LOW//FOUNDED//GIRL SCOUTS//1912" and was available for seven years. It sold for $6.50 and was packed in a clear plastic display box.

2½" heavy painted English metal figurine of Lady Baden-Powell wearing a dark blue suit and hat and her famous "Fish" award. It is unmarked. $75.00.

2¼" painted English metal figurine of Girl Scout wears the khaki uniform from 1920 – 1928 era. Price not available. Courtesy Carolyn Nestrick.

6" wooden nodders from Japan show a Brownie, two Girl Scouts, and a Boy Scout. All have painted features and clothing. $100.00 each.

Trio of Japanese wooden nodders, a Girl Scout, Brownie, and smaller Brownie with painted-on clothing and features. $100.00 each. *Courtesy Carolyn Nestrick.*

Wooden Japanese nodders are painted to portray Japanese Scout and Brownie, each with painted features and clothing. $75.00. *Courtesy Judith Izen.*

4½" wooden jointed movable figurine is marked "W. Germany," has painted features and painted clothes. Fish is made of plastic; figurine, $15.00.

2½" resin Girl Scout Bear figurine by one of the largest Girl Scout cookie manufacturers made as a sample incentive for Girl Scout cookie sales, $15.00. *Courtesy Lynne Armstrong.*

Swaps

Creative collectors make craft items to exchange at gatherings as small favors or as gifts for friends. They are often referred to as swaps.

Set of three 3" wooden clothespin Girl Scout dolls handcrafted by Mary Eskridge as favors. Painted clothes and synthetic hair tied with a ribbon. Not official. *Courtesy of Carolyn Nestrick collection.*

Set of three 5½" to 6½" cloth Girl Scout dolls handcrafted by Mary Eskridge. They have synthetic curly hair, using Girl Scout material for costumes, but are not official.

5½" wooden handcrafted Brownie favor made by Anna Vega has painted features, synthetic hair, cloth vest and trim, and is not official.

Cake Decorations

3" to 4" plastic and porcelain figurines probably used as cake decorations show four stages of Scouting, Brownie, Junior, Cadette, and Senior from the 1950s, 1960s, and 1970s. Some of the figurines are marked "Made in Japan," and some were carried by Wilton during the 1960s. $10.00+. Courtesy of the Sutton, Nestrick, and Armstrong collections.

2" clay dough handmade Brownies have molded, painted hair and features. They have molded-on clothing, brown dotted shirts with orange ties, brown jumpers and sashes, and dark brown hats.
Courtesy Carolyn Nestrick collection.

4" Girl Scout and Brownie pair made of Sculpey-type material with painted, molded features wear cotton costumes. $65.00+. Courtesy Gail Schrader.

1½" chalk figures used as cake decorations, Brownie, Cadette, Intermediate, and Leader, $20.00 each. Courtesy Lynne Armstrong.

3¾" plastic Cracker Jack Girl Scouts found as prizes in Cracker Jack boxes. They came in green, yellow, blue, white, and black; $20.00+. Courtesy Carolyn Nestrick collection.

New 3¾" plastic unmarked Christmas ornaments originally had loop on head to hang on tree. No price available. Courtesy Pidd Miller.

2½" plastic Girl Scout and Brownie figures have jointed arms and are probably also cake decorations; $20.00+. Courtesy Lynne Armstrong.

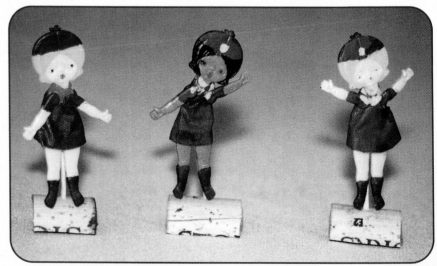

Paper Dolls

Paper dolls from the early part of the twentieth century can be found in magazines such as *Ladies' Home Journal* and later in others like *Jack and Jill* and *The Golden Magazine*. Sheila Young created a whole series of paper doll characters and their wardrobes in the 1920s, and one of them was Polly Pratt who had an adventure as a Camp Fire Girl. Other sources of paper dolls were the Sunday comic section of newspapers.

Reproduction 9" x 12" book of Sheila Young's 6" Polly Pratt paper dolls has a page, "Polly Pratt Goes to a Vacation Camp and Meets Janey Taylor." On this page Janey has a two-piece tan bloomer Camp Fire Girls uniform with matching hat and a navy and white uniform, circa 1920s. This is a Dover publication published in 1992 and sold for $4.95.

This early 6" paper doll by unknown maker has the khaki uniform of 1918 – 1928. The hat for the uniform is missing. Framed it makes a great wall-hanging, $15.00.

An 11" x 16" page from the Ladies' Home Journal February 1917 issue, shows a 5½" Betty Bonnet's Camp-Fire Cousin by artist Sheila Young. Young pictures a brown two-piece Camp Fire Girl bloomer style costume and a fringed Indian dress with symbols for special Camp Fire meetings. $40.00.

Polly Pratt Goes to a Vacation Camp and Meets Janey Taylor is a reproduction of the original Sheila Young paper doll that appeared in June of 1920.

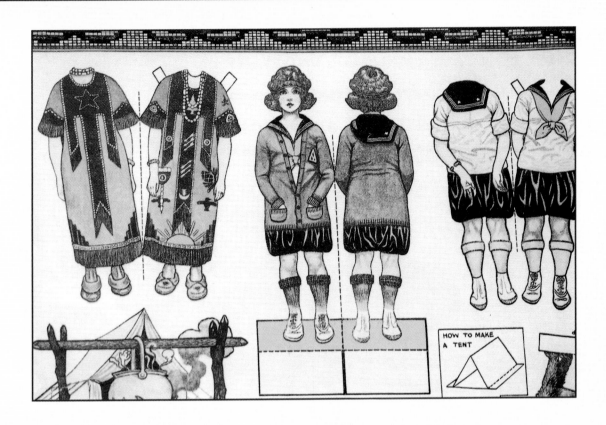

McCall's magazine in August of 1922 had this 11" x 16" page of paper dolls that show two sides to each figure. Titled "Strike Out for the Camp-Fire Trail!" by Mel Cummin, it includes a 4½" paper doll with dark bloomer-style shorts, a fringed Indian style dress, a short pleated shirt with white blouse, a canoe, paddle, dog, and tent. $40.00.

This Dover book, Tom Tierney's *American Family of the 1920s*, contains a paper doll page showing clothing for a 1920s 9" Camp Fire Girl in camp-style uniform with white shirt, red tie, navy bloomer-style shorts, and navy knee-high stockings. This book was published in 1988 and sold for $4.95.

Paper doll book by artist Tom Tierney, Notable American Women shows a 20½" Juliette Low in a group of three women on the cover. Juliette is on the left wearing a blue and black empire style gown. Inside the book, she is shown with this same gown and a matching black hat. Also Juliette is shown with her two-piece brown Girl Scout uniform with matching hat. The book was published in 1989 by Dover Publications and sold for $4.95 new; today's price, $8.00 – 10.00.

In 1994, Kathryn McMurtry Hunt wrote Volume I of "On My Honor," a paper doll history of the Girls Scouts through the eyes of a girl who belonged to the first troop. Lynette C. Ross illustrated it. The paper doll book takes a look at Scouting using paper dolls from March 12, 1912 to October 31, 1927. When issued, the cost was $8.95.

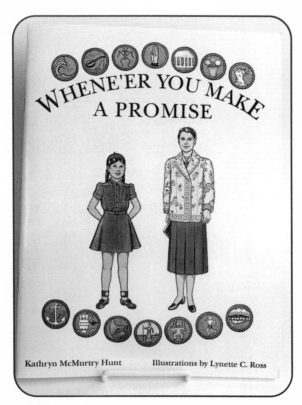

In 1996, Kathryn McMurtry published "Whene'er You Make A Promise," Volume II, a paper doll history of the Girl Scouts from July 1, 1929 to December 28, 1941. Lynette C. Ross illustrated it. It orginally sold for $9.95. This volume and the first one by McMurtry on page 145 are great resources for the Scout paper doll collector.

This 6½" paper doll is from the late 1930s or early 1940s on heavy cardboard, probably from a Girl Scout cookie box. It pictures a Girl Scout green uniform with long sleeves, one pocket on bodice, and two on skirt. There is a matching green hat and a yellow tie. $50.00+.

In July of 1945, the children's magazine Jack and Jill featured a 6" Girl Scout Leader and 5" Brownie paper doll. The Leader wears her long-sleeved dress with matching hat, and the Brownie has a short-sleeved brown dress with pocket on the bodice and dark brown beanie style hat. She also has shorts, a shirt, and sweater. $30.00. *Courtesy Lynne Armstrong.*

6¾" "Bertha as a Brownie" is from the color comic section of a newspaper. Even though the color of the uniform is green, the text reads, "Bertha is a Brownie. She will help the Scouts in the Memorial Day exercises." From the style of the hat, this would date Bertha in the late 1930s or early 1940s. $50.00+. *Carolyn Nestrick collection, photo Lynne Armstrong.*

These Girl Scout and Brownie paper dolls seated by a campfire are from a 1950s cookie box. The knife cut-out has a blade that will open and close. These were given to the author by her Girl Scout sister, Mary Eskridge. No price available.

The January 1949 Jack and Jill children's magazine has a 5½" Girl Scout Dressmaker Paper Doll as the centerfold. This paper doll gives directions on how to draw and decorate your own clothes for her. The magazine originally cost 25¢ a copy, today's price, $30.00.

The 6¾" Brownie paper doll is from the late 1940s on a 4" x 7½" heavy cardboard from a Girl Scout cookie box. $50.00+. Complete set courtesy Lynne Armstrong.

This Girl Scout paper doll is from the late 1940s and is printed on heavy cardboard from a Girl Scout cookie box. She is missing her hat and possibly a purse. The strips of pictures above and below her are from the sides of the box. The paper doll is shown with a striped T-shirt and shorts and has a long-sleeved green dress with yellow tie and long-sleeved green cardigan, $50.00+.

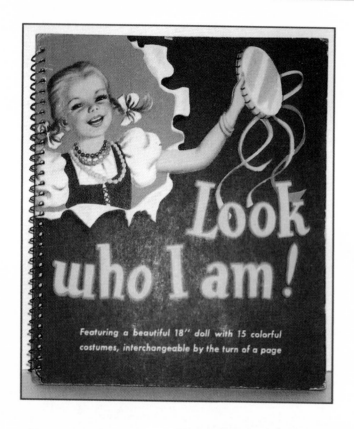

Look Who I Am! is a wonderful paper doll book with the doll built in on the back cover. You unfold the head and legs to make an 18" paper doll. By turning the pages of the book, you can dress her in 15 different costumes and have a little rhyme to go with each. It was written by Rosemary Shawn, illustrated by Doris Stolberg, and published by Hart Publishing Company, New York, in 1952. The Girl Scout page reads: "I'm a helpful Girl Scout; we have a special group. It's fun to be a member of our little Girl Scout Troop. We do a good deed daily – give help to everyone. We sing and play and make nice things and just have loads of fun!" $65.00.

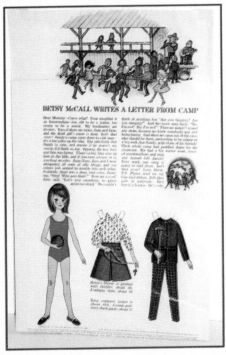

Betsy McCall was first introduced as a paper doll on a single page in May of 1951 in McCall's magazine and continued until the late 1970s. The paper doll page chronicles the fashion styles for girls during this time period. Betsy was a modern girl and partici-pated in many activities including being a Girl Scout. The first artist was Kay Morrisy, followed by Ginnie Hoffman in August 1958. Selma Robins wrote most of the short stories included with the paper dolls. Four different Scout paper dolls have been found; 6" Betsy McCall does a good turn, 1956; 5½" Betsy McCall, Junior Girl Scout, March 1965; 5½" Betsy McCall writes a letter from camp, 1965; and 5" Betsy McCall finds a place in the woods, September, 1973. These paper dolls are official and priced from $5.00 to $15.00.

The first commercially made Girl Scout paper dolls were produced by De Journette Mfg. Company of Atlanta, Georgia. The 1951 catalog shows the boxed set of Girl Scout and Brownie dolls with "real" hair, "The aristocrat of paper dolls." They had 29 uniforms of members in the World Association of Girls Scouts and Girl Guides. They sold for 79 cents each with extra dolls 20 cents each. Paper dolls are a good buy now for collectors; however, mint uncut dolls always bring the highest prices.

Brownie Scout Paper Doll by De Journette Mfg. Company of Atlanta, Georgia, circa 1951 – 1954, features stand-up doll with "real" blonde hair, tan dress and cap, brown shoes and socks. The red and white package features a see-through window and Girl Scout logo on the cover. The catalog number is 11-951. The paper doll is 8¾" tall. The companion Girl Scout paper doll has a green dress with gold tie. The green and white package features a see-through window and Girl Scout logo on the cover. The catalog number is 11-946. The package measures 6½" by 10" and was marked 79¢; today, $25.00+. Bottom left set was available from 1955 through 1960 and had 39 uniforms.

Girl Scout Paper Doll, circa 1961, features stand-up doll that no longer has "real" hair, it is printed. No maker is identified, marked only, "Made in U.S.A." The Girl Scout has a green dress, hat, and gold tie. There were now 44 official uniforms of foreign nations which sold for 65¢ with extra dolls, black, Asian, and Hispanic, for 20¢. The paper doll is 8¾" tall. $25.00+.

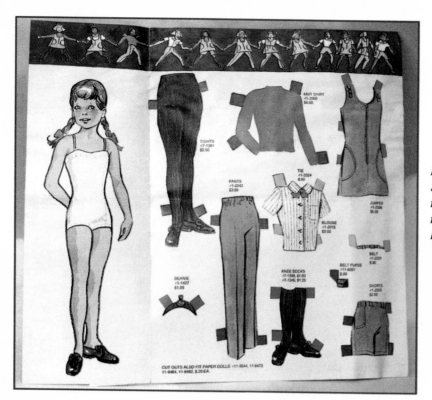

From 1973 to 1986, the GSUSA National Equipment Service offered the Brownie paper dolls with the new mix 'n match Brownie uniform to advertise and promote this new Brownie uniform, $20.00. Courtesy Lynne Armstrong.

The 1970 9" Girl Scout and Brownie paper dolls still came in a clear plastic bag with no maker identified, only marked, "Made in U.S.A." They no longer had a count of the uniforms in the bag and extra dolls; white, black, Asian, and Hispanic were still available. The dolls sold for 20¢ and the bag of uniforms with doll for $1.25. Today the price is $25.00+.

In July 1965 The Golden Magazine, another children's publication, there is a "Girl Scout Roundup" story by Helen Jensen and a 7" Sally Senior Girl Scout paper doll by Neva Schultz. Sally has all the clothes she will need for the Roundup. The annual subscription to the magazine was $4.00. Today's price for the Scout memorabilia, $30.00.

Upper and lower right and opposite page: "Schoolgirls" paper dolls by James and Jonathan, Inc., were available in 1964/1965, and each book had two paper dolls and their Brownie uniforms and other outfits. The 8" paper dolls were named Wendy, Robin, Jane, Winifred, and Jan. They originally sold for 10¢. The dolls have their initials on the tabs on their clothes. Price of uncut book, $25.00+. Robin and Wendy paper dolls courtesy Lynne Armstrong.

Robin   Wendy

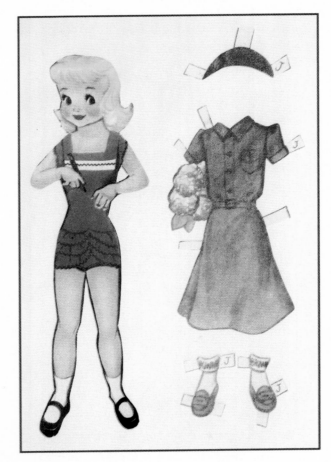

Still sealed in the 11" x 17" package, this 1987 Girl Scout game has four 5" Girl Scout cut-outs, neighbors in the house, man and woman, senior citizens, young man, teenage boy, little boy, Juliette Low, and a dog. This game was to teach young girls how to sell the cookies. This was made available to the Girl Scout Leaders from the cookie manufacturer, Burry-Lu.

This Gilda Radner paper doll book measures 9" x 12" and shows a 10½" Gilda as a Brownie Scout. It was copyrighted September 1979 by Avon Books and sold for $2.95; today's price is $10.00 – 20.00.

Four fiberboard Carousel Kids paper dolls, ranging in size from 4" to 6", were available from the Girl Scouts in 1996/1997. The dolls have Velcro to which the clothes attach. A rack holds the wardrobe. Shown is a complete set; these paper dolls have been discontinued. Doll from $4.75; clothing from $4.25.

This cute little cardboard cylinder novelty is 20" tall, 24" in circumference, and has a plastic removable cap and metal bottom. It was offered in the Girl Scout catalogs. The doll wears a brown uniform with an orange tie and holds a first aid booklet in one hand. This was official circa 1972. $75.00.

Official Girl Scout Pins

Girl Scout pins containing figures have been found starting circa the 1940s through the late 1970s. These pins are very collectible among Girl Scout enthusiasts. Most of the pins are made of a plastic material with a couple of cloth variations. They have a metal pin-type closure on the back. These pins were official and sold in Girl Scout National Equipment catalogs. They measure in size from 1" to 2" and were meant to be worn on everyday clothing, not uniforms. All pins shown are courtesy of Mary Eskridge.

Circa 1940, a 1⅞ x ⅝" hard plastic Girl Scout with long-sleeved green dress, matching hat, and bouquet of flowers, $125.00.

Circa 1940, a standing hard plastic 1¾" x ⅝" Brownie wearing short-sleeved brown dress with matching hat, $125.00.

Circa 1940 – 1944, 1¾" x 1⅛" hard plastic head of Girl Scout with painted features, green hat, and red tie, $45.00.

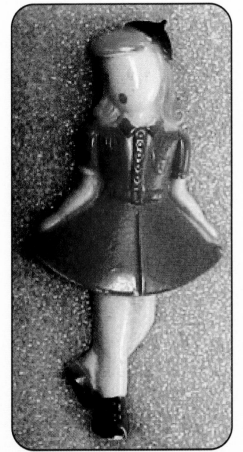

Circa 1941 – 1944, 1⅞" x 1" hard plastic Brownie in short-sleeved dress and hat, curtsying, $75.00.

Cloth over metal variation pin, 2" x 1⅜", of Brownie, circa 1943 – 1944, $75.00.

Cloth over metal pin, 1¾" x 1¼" Girl Scout with green hat and yellow tie; pink and gold frame is circa 1943 – 1947, $50.00.

2⅛" x 1½" hard plastic Girl Scout in green dress, hat, and socks with red tie and backpack carries a brown walking stick, from the 1944 – 1948 era and priced at $45.00.

2" x 1" hard plastic Brownie with short-sleeved brown dress and hat, carries a red over-the-shoulder purse, wears roller skates, and dates circa 1944 – 1946. $45.00.

Circa 1952 – 1956, this 1¾" x 1⅛" hard plastic Brownie pin may often be found with a broken pigtail, $40.00.

This 1⅞" x 1" hard plastic pin from the 1953 era shows a Brownie with short-sleeved brown dress, hat, and shoes playing with her spotted terrier-type dog, $40.00.

A 2¼" x 1¼" hard plastic Girl Scout pin, circa 1948 – 1951, with long-sleeved green dress and hat is shown with her black and white spotted Dalmatian making this a dual collectible for Dalmatian and Scout collectors, $40.00.

This 2" x ¾" hard plastic Brownie pin with short-sleeved brown dress, hat, and shoes is holding a tan cat from the 1954 – 1958 era, $40.00.

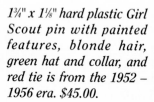

1¾" x 1⅛" hard plastic Girl Scout pin with painted features, blonde hair, green hat and collar, and red tie is from the 1952 – 1956 era. $45.00.

1⅞" x 1⅞" hard plastic trefoil emblem with Girl Scout with green hat, green collar, and red tie, painted features, brown hair, green eyes, and open/closed smiling mouth with teeth, circa 1959 – 1962, $45.00.

This 2⅛" x 1" hard plastic pin of a Girl Scout with long-sleeved green dress, hat, and socks is holding a green Girl Scout banner from the 1956 – 1959 era, $45.00.

There are subtle differences in these three hard plastic Brownie pins. One has no tie at the neck, one has a tie at the neck, and the other has a striped collar.

This 1⅞" x 1¼" hard plastic pin of Brownie with red bow dates from the 1958 – 1962 era; it has no tie at the neck, $35.00.

This 1⅞" x 1¼" hard plastic Brownie pin with red does have a tie at the neck and dates from 1962 – 1973, $30.00.

Final 1⅞" x 1¼" hard plastic Brownie pin with striped collar dates from the 1973 – 1979 era and is priced $30.00.

Stuffed Animals

There have been a large number of Scout related stuffed animals available over the years — here are just a few.

The 10" acrylic plush brown and white bear with foam stuffing wears an orange ribbon stamped "Brownies" and was available in the 1984/1985 Girl Scout USA catalog, #11-137 for $8.50. The hand puppet bear with the green ribbon was available in the 1996/1997 Girl Scout USA catalog.

This 11" plush bear with cookie can wears a 1992 "Rainbow of Fun" T-shirt from the San Jacinto Girl Scouts. Shirt courtesy Pidd Miller.

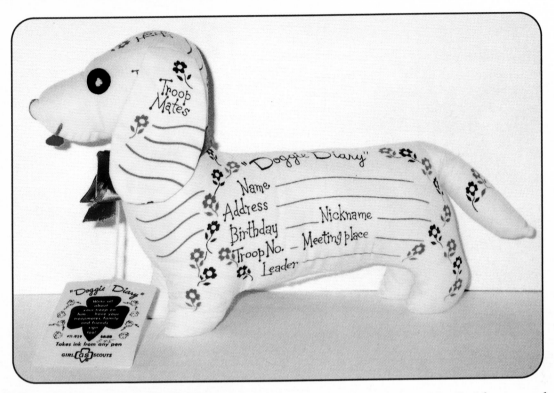

Shown in the mid-1960s Girl Scout catalogs is the yellow gabardine "Doggie Diary" with green and brown printing. It was designed to be written on with pens. The dog is 15" long and stands 8" tall. He originally sold for $3.50; today's price, $50.00.

The 15" white Autograph Hound was available circa 1997 and the green ribbon around his necks reads, "I love Girl Scouts;" he was an incentive gift for cookie sales.

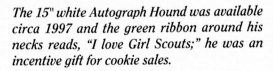

These 8" plush jointed bears are dressed to resemble Girl Scouts and Brownies and are available from Juliette Low's birthplace in Savannah. Mary Meyer, who also does the Girl Scout Beaners, makes them. They were not available in the regular Girl Scout catalog and are Junior Girl Scout, Cadette, Khaki Uniform, Brownie, Daisy, and Senior, $10.00 each.

These jointed 12" plush bears are from the 1997/1998 Girl Scout catalog and also have accessory glasses available. They are Daisy (blue), Brownie, and Junior (green). They sold for $15.00 each.

In the 2000/2001 Girl Scout catalog, a new 11" Cadette bear was introduced which sells for $15.00.

Four velour "Belly Beans," 7" – 9" animals, are the Girl Scout Beaners. A blue cat is Cadette & Senior, a brown bear is a Brownie, a blue and white cow is Daisy, and a green dog represents a Junior Scout. Mary Meyer Corporation, Townshead, Vermont, makes these bears.

The plush 3½" Garfield was a Girl Scout cookie incentive and on his shirt it says, "I eat Girl Scout Cookies one box at a time."

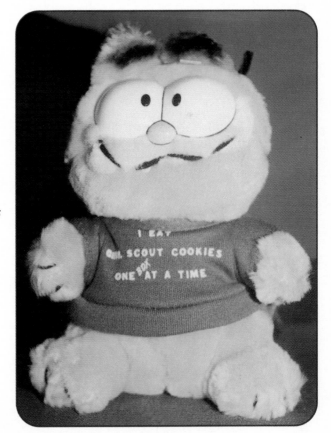

Bibliography

Anderton, Johanna Gast, *The Collector's Encyclopedia of Cloth Dolls*, Wallace Homestead Book Co., 1984.

Axe, John, *Effanbee, A Collector's Encyclopedia 1949 through 1983*, Hobby House Press, 1983.

Bourgeois, Joseph G. *Dolls in Uniform*, Collector Books, 1995.

Casper, Peggy Wiedman, *Fashionable Terri Lee Dolls*, Hobby House Press, 1988.

Degenhardt, Mary and Judith Kirsch, *Girl Scout Collecting Guide*, Wallace Homestead, 1987.

Edward, Linda, *Cloth Dolls, Antique to Modern*, Schiffer Publishing, 1997.

Izen, Judith and Carol Stover, *Vogue Dolls*, Collector Books, 1998.

Judd, Polly and Pam Judd, *Hard Plastic Dolls, I*, Hobby House Press, 1985.
         Hard Plastic Dolls, II, Hobby House Press, 1989.

Moyer, Patsy, *Doll Values*, Collector Books, 1997 – 2002.

Niswonger, Jeanne DuChateau, *That Doll Ginny*, Cody Publications, 1978.

Pace, Mildred Mastin et al, *Juliette Low*, Jesse Stuart Foundation, 1997.

Shultz, Gladys Denny and Lawrence Shultz, *Daisy Gordon, Lady From Savannah*, Girls Scouts of the USA, 1980.

Girl Scout National Equipment Catalogs, 1929 – 2001.

Other

American Girl Magazine published by Girl Scouts, July, November, 1935.

Doll Reader, "Pied Piperess: Grace Corry Rockwell and Her Beautiful Children," Mary Lou Ratcliff, November 1989.

Gordon Family Papers, Library of the University of North Carolina at Chapel Hill.

Index

COLLECTOR BOOKS
informing today's collector

www.collectorbooks.com

For over two decades we have been keeping collectors informed on trends and values in all fields of antiques and collectibles.

DOLLS, FIGURES & TEDDY BEARS

4631	**Barbie Doll** Boom, 1986–1995, Augustyniak	$18.95
2079	**Barbie Doll** Fashion, Volume I, Eames	$24.95
4846	**Barbie Doll** Fashion, Volume II, Eames	$24.95
3957	**Barbie** Exclusives, Rana	$18.95
4632	**Barbie** Exclusives, Book II, Rana	$18.95
6022	The **Barbie Doll** Years, 5th Ed., Olds	$19.95
3810	**Chatty Cathy** Dolls, Lewis	$15.95
5352	Collector's Ency. of **Barbie** Doll Exclusives & More, 2nd Ed., Augustyniak	$24.95
4863	Collector's Encyclopedia of **Vogue Dolls**, Izen/Stover	$29.95
5904	Collector's Guide to **Celebrity Dolls**, Spurgeon	$24.95
5599	Collector's Guide to **Dolls of the 1960s and 1970s**, Sabulis	$24.95
6030	Collector's Guide to **Horsman Dolls**, Jensen	$29.95
6025	**Doll Values**, Antique to Modern, 6th Ed., Moyer	$12.95
6033	**Modern Collectible Dolls**, Volume VI, Moyer	$24.95
5689	**Nippon Dolls** & Playthings, Van Patten/Lau	$29.95
5365	**Peanuts Collectibles**, Podley/Bang	$24.95
6026	**Small Dolls of the 40s & 50s**, Stover	$29.95
5253	Story of **Barbie**, 2nd Ed., Westenhouser	$24.95
5277	**Talking Toys** of the 20th Century, Lewis	$15.95
2084	**Teddy Bears, Annalee's & Steiff** Animals, 3rd Series, Mandel	$19.95
1808	Wonder of **Barbie**, Manos	$9.95
1430	World of **Barbie** Dolls, Manos	$9.95
4880	World of **Raggedy Ann** Collectibles, Avery	$24.95

TOYS & MARBLES

2333	Antique & Collectible **Marbles**, 3rd Ed., Grist	$9.95
4559	Collectible **Action Figures**, 2nd Ed., Manos	$17.95
5900	Collector's Guide to **Battery Toys**, 2nd Edition, Hultzman	$24.95
4566	Collector's Guide to **Tootsietoys**, 2nd Ed., Richter	$19.95
5169	Collector's Guide to **TV Toys** & Memorabilia, 2nd Ed., Davis/Morgan	$24.95
5593	Grist's Big Book of **Marbles**, 2nd Ed.	$24.95
3970	Grist's Machine-Made & Contemporary **Marbles**, 2nd Ed.	$9.95
5267	**Matchbox Toys**, 1947 to 1998, 3rd Ed., Johnson	$19.95
5830	**McDonald's** Collectibles, 2nd Edition, Henriques/DuVall	$24.95
5673	Modern **Candy Containers** & Novelties, Brush/Miller	$19.95
1540	Modern **Toys** 1930–1980, Baker	$19.95
5920	**Schroeder's Collectible Toys**, Antique to Modern Price Guide, 8th Ed.	$17.95
5908	**Toy Car** Collector's Guide, Johnson	$19.95

FURNITURE

3716	American **Oak** Furniture, Book II, McNerney	$12.95
1118	Antique **Oak** Furniture, Hill	$7.95
3720	Collector's Encyclopedia of **American** Furniture, Vol. III, Swedberg	$24.95
5359	Early **American** Furniture, Obbard	$12.95
3906	**Heywood-Wakefield** Modern Furniture, Rouland	$18.95
1885	**Victorian** Furniture, Our American Heritage, McNerney	$9.95
3829	**Victorian** Furniture, Our American Heritage, Book II, McNerney	$9.95

JEWELRY, HATPINS, WATCHES & PURSES

4704	Antique & Collectible **Buttons**, Wisniewski	$19.95
1748	Antique **Purses**, Revised Second Ed., Holiner	$19.95
4850	Collectible **Costume Jewelry**, Simonds	$24.95
5675	Collectible **Silver Jewelry**, Rezazadeh	$24.95
3722	Collector's Ency. of **Compacts**, Carryalls & Face Powder Boxes, Mueller	$24.95
4940	**Costume Jewelry**, A Practical Handbook & Value Guide, Rezazadeh	$24.95
5812	Fifty Years of Collectible **Fashion Jewelry**, 1925–1975, Baker	$24.95
1424	**Hatpins** & Hatpin Holders, Baker	$9.95
5695	**Ladies' Vintage Accessories**, Bruton	$24.95
1181	100 Years of Collectible **Jewelry**, 1850–1950, Baker	$9.95
4729	**Sewing Tools** & Trinkets, Thompson	$24.95
6038	**Sewing Tools** & Trinkets, Volume 2, Thompson	$24.95
6039	Signed Beauties of **Costume Jewelry**, Brown	$24.95
5620	Unsigned Beauties of **Costume Jewelry**, Brown	$24.95
4878	Vintage & Contemporary **Purse Accessories**, Gerson	$24.95
5696	Vintage & Vogue Ladies' **Compacts**, 2nd Edition, Gerson	$29.95
5923	**Vintage Jewelry** for Investment & Casual Wear, Edeen	$24.95

INDIANS, GUNS, KNIVES, TOOLS, PRIMITIVES

6021	**Arrowheads** of the Central Great Plains, Fox	$19.95
1868	Antique **Tools**, Our American Heritage, McNerney	$9.95
5616	Big Book of **Pocket Knives**, Stewart	$19.95
4943	Field Guide to Flint **Arrowheads** & **Knives** of the North American Indian	$9.95
3885	**Indian Artifacts** of the Midwest, Book II, Hothem	$16.95
4870	**Indian Artifacts** of the Midwest, Book III, Hothem	$18.95
5685	**Indian Artifacts** of the Midwest, Book IV, Hothem	$19.95
6132	**Modern Guns**, Identification & Values, 14th Ed., Quertermous	$14.95
2164	**Primitives**, Our American Heritage, McNerney	$9.95
1759	**Primitives**, Our American Heritage, 2nd Series, McNerney	$14.95
6031	Standard **Knife** Collector's Guide, 4th Ed., Ritchie & Stewart	$14.95
5999	**Wilderness** Survivor's Guide, Hamper	$12.95

PAPER COLLECTIBLES & BOOKS

4633	**Big Little Books**, Jacobs	$18.95
5902	**Boys' & Girls' Book** Series	$19.95
4710	Collector's Guide to **Children's Books**, 1850 to 1950, Volume I, Jones	$18.95
5153	Collector's Guide to **Children's Books**, 1850 to 1950, Volume II, Jones	$19.95
1441	Collector's Guide to **Post Cards**, Wood	$9.95
5926	**Duck Stamps**, Chappell	$9.95
2081	Guide to Collecting **Cookbooks**, Allen	$14.95
2080	Price Guide to **Cookbooks & Recipe Leaflets**, Dickinson	$9.95
3973	**Sheet Music** Reference & Price Guide, 2nd Ed., Pafik & Guiheen	$19.95
6041	Vintage **Postcards for the Holidays**, Reed	$24.95
4733	**Whitman Juvenile Books**, Brown	$17.95

GLASSWARE

5602	Anchor Hocking's **Fire-King** & More, 2nd Ed.	$24.95
5823	Collectible **Glass Shoes**, 2nd Edition, Wheatley	$24.95
5897	Coll. **Glassware** from the 40s, 50s & 60s, 6th Ed., Florence	$19.95
1810	Collector's Encyclopedia of **American Art Glass**, Shuman	$29.95
5907	Collector's Encyclopedia of **Depression Glass**, 15th Ed., Florence	$19.95
1961	Collector's Encyclopedia of **Fry Glassware**, Fry Glass Society	$24.95
1664	Collector's Encyclopedia of **Heisey Glass**, 1925–1938, Bredehoft	$24.95
3905	Collector's Encyclopedia of **Milk Glass**, Newbound	$24.95
4936	Collector's Guide to **Candy Containers**, Dezso/Poirier	$19.95
5820	Collector's Guide to **Glass Banks**, Reynolds	$24.95
4564	**Crackle Glass**, Weitman	$19.95
4941	**Crackle Glass**, Book II, Weitman	$19.95
4714	**Czechoslovakian Glass** and Collectibles, Book II, Barta/Rose	$16.95
5528	Early American **Pattern Glass**, Metz	$17.95
6125	**Elegant Glassware** of the Depression Era, 10th Ed., Florence	$24.95
3981	Evers' Standard **Cut Glass** Value Guide	$12.95
5614	Field Guide to **Pattern Glass**, McCain	$17.95
5615	Florence's **Glassware Pattern Identification** Guide, Vol. II	$19.95

19	**Fostoria**, Etched, Carved & Cut Designs, Vol. II, Kerr	$24.95
61	**Fostoria Tableware**, 1924 – 1943, Long/Seate	$24.95
61	**Fostoria Tableware**, 1944 – 1986, Long/Seate	$24.95
04	**Fostoria**, Useful & Ornamental, Long/Seate	$29.95
99	Glass & Ceramic **Baskets**, White	$19.95
44	**Imperial Carnival Glass**, Burns	$18.95
27	**Kitchen Glassware** of the Depression Years, 6th Ed., Florence	$24.95
00	Much More Early American **Pattern Glass**, Metz	$17.95
45	**Northwood Carnival Glass**, 1908 – 1925, Burns	$19.95
36	Pocket Guide to **Depression Glass**, 13th Ed., Florence	$12.95
23	Standard Encyclopedia of **Carnival Glass**, 8th Ed., Edwards/Carwile	$29.95
24	Standard **Carnival Glass** Price Guide, 13th Ed., Edwards/Carwile	$9.95
35	Standard Encyclopedia of **Opalescent Glass**, 4th Ed., Edwards/Carwile	$24.95
32	**Very Rare Glassware** of the Depression Years, 5th Series, Florence	$24.95

POTTERY

27	**ABC Plates & Mugs**, Lindsay	$24.95
29	**American Art Pottery**, Sigafoose	$24.95
30	**American Limoges**, Limoges	$24.95
12	**Blue & White Stoneware**, McNerney	$9.95
59	**Blue Willow**, 2nd Ed., Gaston	$14.95
51	Collectible **Cups & Saucers**, Harran	$18.95
73	Collector's Encyclopedia of **American Dinnerware**, Cunningham	$24.95
31	Collector's Encyclopedia of **Bauer Pottery**, Chipman	$24.95
34	Collector's Encyclopedia of **California Pottery**, 2nd Ed., Chipman	$24.95
23	Collector's Encyclopedia of **Cookie Jars**, Book II, Roerig	$24.95
39	Collector's Encyclopedia of **Cookie Jars**, Book III, Roerig	$24.95
48	Collector's Encyclopedia of **Fiesta**, 9th Ed., Huxford	$24.95
61	Collector's Encyclopedia of **Early Noritake**, Alden	$24.95
12	Collector's Encyclopedia of **Flow Blue China**, 2nd Ed., Gaston	$24.95
31	Collector's Encyclopedia of **Homer Laughlin China**, Jasper	$24.95
76	Collector's Encyclopedia of **Hull Pottery**, Roberts	$19.95
62	Collector's Encyclopedia of **Lefton China**, DeLozier	$19.95
55	Collector's Encyclopedia of **Lefton China**, Book II, DeLozier	$19.95
09	Collector's Encyclopedia of **Limoges Porcelain**, 3rd Ed., Gaston	$29.95
34	Collector's Encyclopedia of **Majolica Pottery**, Katz-Marks	$19.95
58	Collector's Encyclopedia of **McCoy Pottery**, Huxford	$19.95
77	Collector's Encyclopedia of **Niloak**, 2nd Edition, Gifford	$29.95
37	Collector's Encyclopedia of **Nippon Porcelain**, Van Patten	$24.95
65	Collector's Ency. of **Nippon Porcelain**, 3rd Series, Van Patten	$24.95
53	Collector's Ency. of **Nippon Porcelain**, 5th Series, Van Patten	$24.95
78	Collector's Ency. of **Nippon Porcelain**, 6th Series, Van Patten	$29.95
47	Collector's Encyclopedia of **Noritake**, Van Patten	$19.95
64	Collector's Encyclopedia of **Pickard China**, Reed	$29.95
79	Collector's Encyclopedia of **Red Wing Art Pottery**, Dollen	$24.95
18	Collector's Encyclopedia of **Rosemeade Pottery**, Dommel	$24.95
41	Collector's Encyclopedia of **Roseville Pottery**, Revised, Huxford/Nickel	$24.95
42	Collector's Encyclopedia of **Roseville Pottery**, 2nd Series, Huxford/Nickel	$24.95
17	Collector's Encyclopedia of **Russel Wright**, 3rd Editon, Kerr	$29.95
70	Collector's Encyclopedia of **Stangl Dinnerware**, Runge	$24.95
21	Collector's Encyclopedia of **Stangl Artware**, Lamps, and Birds, Runge	$29.95
14	Collector's Encyclopedia of **Van Briggle Art Pottery**, Sasicki	$24.95
80	Collector's Guide to **Feather Edge Ware**, McAllister	$19.95
76	Collector's Guide to **Lu-Ray Pastels**, Meehan	$18.95
14	Collector's Guide to **Made in Japan Ceramics**, White	$18.95
46	Collector's Guide to **Made in Japan Ceramics**, Book II, White	$18.95
25	**Cookie Jars**, Westfall	$9.95
40	**Cookie Jars**, Book II, Westfall	$19.95
09	**Dresden Porcelain** Studios, Harran	$29.95
18	Florence's Big Book of **Salt & Pepper Shakers**	$24.95

2379	Lehner's Ency. of **U.S. Marks** on Pottery, Porcelain & China	$24.95
4722	**McCoy Pottery**, Collector's Reference & Value Guide, Hanson/Nissen	$19.95
5913	**McCoy Pottery**, Volume III, Hanson & Nissen	$24.95
5691	**Post86 Fiesta**, Identification & Value Guide, Racheter	$19.95
1670	**Red Wing Collectibles**, DePasquale	$9.95
1440	**Red Wing Stoneware**, DePasquale	$9.95
6037	**Rookwood Pottery**, Nicholson & Thomas	$24.95
1632	**Salt & Pepper Shakers**, Guarnaccia	$9.95
5091	**Salt & Pepper Shakers** II, Guarnaccia	$18.95
3443	**Salt & Pepper Shakers** IV, Guarnaccia	$18.95
3738	**Shawnee Pottery**, Mangus	$24.95
4629	Turn of the Century **American Dinnerware**, 1880s–1920s, Jasper	$24.95
3327	**Watt Pottery** – Identification & Value Guide, Morris	$19.95
5924	**Zanesville Stoneware** Company, Rans, Ralston & Russell	$24.95

OTHER COLLECTIBLES

5916	Advertising **Paperweights**, Holiner & Kammerman	$24.95
5838	Advertising **Thermometers**, Merritt	$16.95
5898	Antique & Contemporary **Advertising Memorabilia**, Summers	$24.95
5814	Antique **Brass & Copper** Collectibles, Gaston	$24.95
1880	Antique **Iron**, McNerney	$9.95
3872	Antique **Tins**, Dodge	$24.95
4845	Antique **Typewriters & Office Collectibles**, Rehr	$19.95
5607	Antiquing and Collecting on the **Internet**, Parry	$12.95
1128	**Bottle** Pricing Guide, 3rd Ed., Cleveland	$7.95
3718	Collectible **Aluminum**, Grist	$16.95
5060	Collectible **Souvenir Spoons**, Bednersh	$19.95
5676	Collectible **Souvenir Spoons**, Book II, Bednersh	$29.95
5666	Collector's Encyclopedia of **Granite Ware**, Book 2, Greguire	$29.95
5836	Collector's Guide to **Antique Radios**, 5th Ed., Bunis	$19.95
3966	Collector's Guide to **Inkwells**, Identification & Values, Badders	$18.95
4947	Collector's Guide to **Inkwells**, Book II, Badders	$19.95
5681	Collector's Guide to **Lunchboxes**, White	$19.95
5621	Collector's Guide to **Online Auctions**, Hix	$12.95
4864	Collector's Guide to **Wallace Nutting Pictures**, Ivankovich	$18.95
5683	**Fishing Lure** Collectibles, Vol. 1, Murphy/Edmisten	$29.95
5911	**Flea Market Trader**, 13th Ed., Huxford	$9.95
6227	**Garage Sale** & Flea Market Annual, 11th Edition, Huxford	$19.95
4945	**G-Men and FBI Toys** and Collectibles, Whitworth	$18.95
3819	**General Store** Collectibles, Wilson	$24.95
5912	The **Heddon** Legacy, A Century of Classic **Lures**, Roberts & Pavey	$29.95
2216	**Kitchen Antiques**, 1790–1940, McNerney	$14.95
5991	**Lighting Devices** & Accessories of the 17th – 19th Centuries, Hamper	$9.95
5686	**Lighting Fixtures** of the Depression Era, Book I, Thomas	$24.95
4950	The **Lone Ranger**, Collector's Reference & Value Guide, Felbinger	$18.95
6028	Modern **Fishing Lure** Collectibles, Vol. 1, Lewis	$24.95
6131	Modern **Fishing Lure** Collectibles, Vol. 2, Lewis	$24.95
2026	**Railroad** Collectibles, 4th Ed., Baker	$14.95
5619	**Roy Rogers and Dale Evans** Toys & Memorabilia, Coyle	$24.95
6137	**Schroeder's Antiques** Price Guide, 21st Edition	$14.95
5007	**Silverplated Flatware**, Revised 4th Edition, Hagan	$18.95
6239	**Star Wars** Super Collector's Wish Book, 2nd Ed., Carlton	$29.95
6139	Summers' Guide to **Coca-Cola**, 4th Ed.	$24.95
5905	Summers' Pocket Guide to **Coca-Cola**, 3rd Ed.	$12.95
3977	Value Guide to **Gas Station Memorabilia**, Summers & Priddy	$24.95
4877	Vintage **Bar Ware**, Visakay	$24.95
5925	The Vintage Era of **Golf Club Collectibles**, John	$29.95
6010	The Vintage Era of **Golf Club Collectibles** Collector's Log, John	$9.95
6036	Vintage **Quilts**, Aug, Newman & Roy	$24.95
4935	The W.F. Cody **Buffalo Bill** Collector's Guide with Values	$24.95

This is only a partial listing of the books on antiques that are available from Collector Books. All books are well illustrated and contain current values. Most of these books are available from your local bookseller, antique dealer, or public library. If you are unable to locate certain titles in your area, you may order by mail from **COLLECTOR BOOKS**, P.O. Box 3009, Paducah, KY 42002-3009. Customers with Visa, Master Card, or Discover may phone in orders from 00–5:00 CT, Monday–Friday, Toll Free **1-800-626-5420**, or online at **www.collectorbooks.com**. Add $3.00 for postage for the first book ordered and 50¢ for ach additional book. Include item number, title, and price when ordering. Allow 14 to 21 days for delivery.

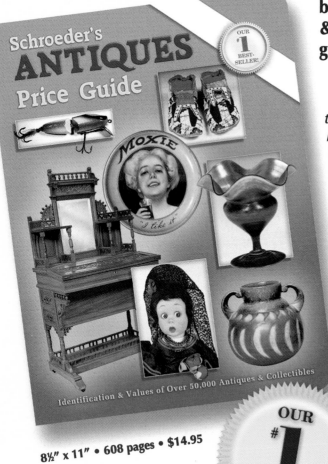